CONFUSION
IN THE
KINGDOM

How "Progressive" Catholicism Is
Bringing Harm and Scandal to the Church

TRENT HORN

Catholic
Answers
Press

Unless otherwise noted, Scripture quotations are from the Revised Standard Version of the Bible, copyright © 1946, 1952, and 1971 National Council of the Churches of Christ in the United States of America. Used by permission. All rights reserved worldwide.

Published by Catholic Answers, Inc.
2020 Gillespie Way
El Cajon, California 92020
1-888-291-8000 orders
619-387-0042 fax
catholic.com

Printed in the United States of America

Cover design by ebooklaunch.com
Interior design by Russell Graphic Design

978-1-68357-347-0
978-1-68357-348-7 Kindle
978-1-68357-349-4 ePub

For Harold and Margie

CONTENTS

INTRODUCTION

"Trent, can you respond to what this Catholic said online? It's just really confusing."

Normally, I don't like to nitpick other Catholics, even if I don't agree with their approach toward sharing our faith. I'm more interested in engaging the arguments of non-Catholic critics like atheists or Protestants who try to disprove the fundamental teachings of the Faith. Or I want to defend the moral teachings of the Church that our culture relentlessly attacks, like its teachings on the sanctity of marriage and human life. I don't want to spend time arguing about matters Catholics are free to disagree about, especially since Scripture condemns this kind of quarreling and infighting. St. Paul said, "Why do you pass judgment on your brother? Or you, why do you despise your brother? For we shall all stand before the judgment seat of God. . . . Let us then pursue what makes for peace and for mutual upbuilding" (Rom. 14:10, 19)

But sometimes fellow believers can confuse the faithful, and when this happens, they must be corrected. Paul even makes this point at the end of his letter to the Romans when he says, "Take note of those who create dissensions and difficulties, in opposition to the doctrine which you have been taught; avoid them. For such persons do not serve our Lord Christ, but their own appetites, and by fair and flattering words they deceive the hearts of the simple-minded" (16:19–21). He also encouraged Timothy to "convince, rebuke, and exhort, be unfailing in patience and in teaching. For the time is coming when people will not endure sound teaching, but having itching ears they will accumulate for themselves teachers to suit their own likings" (2 Tim. 4:2–3).

And though Catholics of any theological leaning can distort the Faith, people usually reach out to me for help when it comes to dissecting the confusion of *liberal* Catholicism. Maybe it's a Catholic author who says Catholics would *really* respect women by not outlawing abortion. Or maybe it's a well-known Catholic priest who says that it's okay to have "gay pride." These public figures don't outright say, "The Church is wrong on abortion and homosexuality," but they do something worse . . . their actions sow seeds of doubt that cause some people to reject the Church's teachings in the name of liberal values like "inclusivity."

So what is liberal Catholicism?

Theological liberalism reached its heyday in the early twentieth century, when, in reaction to the work of German *higher form criticism*, it tried to "modernize" the Christian faith by rejecting doctrines like the Virgin Birth. More conservative Protestants famously countered this movement through the publication of a series of essays called *The Fundamentals: A Testimony to the Truth*, which became the background for later Protestant "fundamentalist" movements.

Similar controversies arose in the Catholic world, with scholars questioning doctrines like papal infallibility (prompting its reaffirmation at Vatican I), the miracle accounts of the Bible, and even foundational teachings like the deity of Christ. One prominent French scholar referred to Jesus as *un homme incomparable*—an incomparable man, but a man nonetheless. Pope Pius X called this primacy of modern sentiments over divine revelation "the synthesis of all heresies" (*Pascendi Dominici Gregis* 39).

It's difficult to define "liberal Catholicism" because the term *liberal* has different meanings. In the nineteenth century, a political "liberal" was someone committed to individual rights, increasing liberty, and limiting government. At the time, the Church condemned this "liberalism" because it failed to acknowledge the legitimate role of the State in guiding people toward not just temporal goods, but spiritual ones as well. Today's liberals, however, are quite happy to enlist the State's help in promoting their understanding of the common good of society. In contrast, those who describe themselves as conservative (and especially libertarians) are the ones most likely to promote limited forms of government.

One way to answer the question is to see how liberal Catholics describe themselves. This also answers critics who say I shouldn't call people "liberals" since the term is akin to a slur—and it may be to some people. But other authors see no problem being called a "liberal Catholic." For example, Michael Sean Winters of the *National Catholic Reporter* says "we liberal Catholics never went away and never could go away."[1] *Reporter* executive editor Heidi Schlumpf gives this description of *liberal* (or, as she says, "progressive") Catholics:

> They are the gray-haired old-timers at church reform organizations and parishes. They are the young Catholics taking their first theology course at a Catholic college or university—and the theologians teaching those classes. They are the retired priests, sisters, and even some bishops who have spent their lives working for social justice. They are Women's March marchers, Green New Deal supporters, and Black Lives Matter protesters across generations.[2]

I'm glad Heidi Schlumpf offers this fairly accurate illustration, because if I did, it would be dismissed as a caricature. Like the liberalism of the nineteenth century, modern Catholic liberals try to reconcile the Church's teachings with modern liberal political values. In particular, I'll focus on the promotion of values that are directly antithetical to the Catholic faith, such as the promotion of abortion, sodomy, and anti-supernaturalism in biblical exegesis. I'll also be criticizing their claims that Catholic social teaching is identical to or even requires alliances with leftist organizations like Black Lives Matter (BLM) and so-called "women's rights" organizations.

But before I continue, I should distinguish liberal Catholics from *far-left* Catholics, or those who openly and unapologetically reject Church teaching on issues like abortion, marriage, and the male priesthood. The central focus of this book is on Catholics who publicly affirm the teachings of the Church but undermine those teachings in their words and deeds.

So when it comes to homosexuality, for example, I won't be spending much time on dissenting priests like Fr. Bryan Massingale who say the Church's teaching on homosexuality is false.[3] Instead, I will be focusing on priests like Fr. James Martin who claim to uphold the Church's teaching on the morality of homosexual acts but then say things that create a cognitive dissonance within people and make them more likely to reject the teaching, such as that there is nothing scandalous about someone in a so-called gay "marriage" teaching at a Catholic school.

Or when it comes to abortion, it's obvious that Catholics for Choice rejects the Church's teaching, so I won't be engaging that group's arguments. But other Catholics, like Emily Reimer-Barry or Stephen Millies, may *say* they accept Church teaching on abortion (in the same way Joe Biden says he accepts it), but their opposition to laws that protect unborn children sows confusion over the teaching. How can the Church teach that abortion is a grave sin of homicide if Catholics should also, according to them, "respect women" or "democracy" by keeping this form of homicide legal?

Second, I should distinguish "liberal Catholics" who confuse the faithful on important teachings from Catholics who simply have more liberal politics. I know Catholics who work tirelessly to make abortion illegal and restore the proper civic definition of marriage but also support government solutions to poverty I find well-intentioned but ultimately ineffective.

And that's okay.

As long as someone affirms what the Church teaches, rejects what the Church opposes, and allows for disagreement on matters the Church has no teaching on, I generally have no qualms with him. But I do have qualms with the liberal Catholics who ignore what is obligatory, celebrate what is evil, and dogmatize what can be a matter of reasonable disagreement.

Of course, conservative and traditional Catholics can be guilty of these same charges, which brings me to the criticism that I should write an entire book on the confusion conservative or traditionalist Catholics create. In fact, I have already addressed "Catholic fundamentalism" on my podcast and in various articles, so I am seriously considering addressing that topic. However, liberal Catholic confusion leads to worse spiritual harms than conservative or traditionalist confusion on Church teaching.

When traditionalist Catholics distort Church teaching, they usually turn the good into the obligatory. The rosary becomes a daily requirement. The Latin Mass becomes the only acceptable liturgy. Or they absolutely forbid even near occasions of sin, like saying movies that depict blasphemy are always wrong to watch. In the worst cases, this rigidity can cause people to lose hope and leave the Church in despair, or become bitter and think they know more than the bishops and fall into the grave sin of schism. But in most cases, it just leads to the venial sin of being annoyingly self-righteous.

Liberal Catholicism, however, is different. Instead of making the good obligatory, it more often makes evil permissible. It sows confusion about whether it's okay to engage in homosexual conduct, have an abortion, or use contraception. And instead of making the permissible forbidden, it more often makes the obligatory optional. It sows confusion about the need to believe in the God revealed in the creeds or the need to protect the unborn from being legally killed. When a Catholic fails to accept the Church's teaching on the death penalty, at worst, he might fall into schism, but odds are he won't go out and participate in an execution. But Catholics who reject Church teaching on abortion, IVF, contraception, or sodomy are far more likely to engage in a moral act that could put them in a state of mortal sin.

Finally, I know that some conservative and traditional Catholics will criticize this book because it doesn't primarily address the confusion surrounding some of Pope Francis's statements or the audacity of what some of the more liberal bishops have said. Though I will be addressing, where the context is appropriate, some of the poor judgments the pope and other bishops have made, readers looking for a catalogue of the controversial statements of Pope Francis and the more outspoken bishops can look to many others who have done that work.

In some cases, emphasizing the perceived failures of the bishops has displaced a vigorous response to the arguments posed by "liberal" or "progressive" Catholic priests and laypeople. This book aims to refocus those counter-arguments, and I hope it encourages other Catholics who care about preserving the deposit of faith from error and scandal to do the same.

PART I

SEX AND LIFE ISSUES

1

"BUILDING BRIDGES"

Have you ever met someone who says something controversial and then acts as though he had said something mundane and wonders why everyone is getting so upset? If not, just follow the work of Fr. James Martin, and you'll have many opportunities to become acquainted with this routine.

For example, on January 21, 2023, the Catholic League tweeted about transportation secretary Pete Buttigieg, widely recognized as married to another man named Chasten, saying, "It is true that Pete Buttigieg is legally married, but that is a legal fiction." Fr. Martin tweeted in response: "Pete Buttigieg is married."[4]

After receiving a torrent of criticism, Fr. Martin published an article where he clarified that all he meant was that "as much as anyone in this country whose marriage [is] registered in City Hall, he and his husband Chasten are legally married."[5] But this is disingenuous because the tweet Fr. Martin originally responded to said Pete and Chasten were legally married. What the Catholic League meant is that the relationship between these men is a marriage *in name only.*

Just as totalitarian states can *say* their citizens have "freedom," but it is fictional freedom that bears no resemblance to the real thing, the state can *say* two men, or three women, or a man and a robot (or who knows what else in the future) can be "married," even though these relationships bear no resemblance to the real thing—to marriage.

Before I explain what else is wrong with this (and many other things Fr. Martin says), it will be helpful to have some backstory on his work involving those who identify as "LGBT."

A Bridge Too Far

Prior to 2016, Fr. Martin was best known as a Catholic commenter who would appear on television shows like *The Colbert Report*. Although he emphasized things like social justice, Martin's work focused on general spirituality and wasn't very controversial. He began to openly court controversy after accepting the "Bridge Building Award" from New Ways Ministry in 2016.

New Ways Ministry openly dissents against the Church's teachings on a variety of issues, including homosexuality. Sr. Jeannine Gramick and Fr. Robert Nugent founded the group in 1977. By 1999, the Congregation (now Dicastery) for the Doctrine of the Faith (CDF, now DDF) noted how the pair "promote ambiguous positions on homosexuality and explicitly criticized documents of the Church's Magisterium on this issue." The CDF said Gramick's and Nugent's statements were "incompatible with the teaching of the Church" and permanently prohibited them from engaging in "any pastoral work involving homosexual persons," insisting that they "are ineligible, for an undetermined period, for any office in their respective religious institutes."[6]

Ten years later, the president of the United States Conference of Catholic Bishops (USCCB), Cardinal Francis George, issued a clarification of the status of New Ways Ministry:

> No one should be misled by the claim that New Ways Ministry provides an authentic interpretation of Catholic teaching and an authentic Catholic pastoral practice. Their claim to be Catholic only confuses the faithful regarding the authentic teaching and ministry of the Church with respect to persons with a homosexual inclination. Accordingly, I wish to make it clear that, like other groups that claim to be Catholic but deny central aspects of Church teaching, New Ways Ministry has no approval or recognition from the Catholic Church and that they cannot speak on behalf of the Catholic faithful in the United States.[7]

Just as it would be scandalous for me to accept an award related to apologetics from a group of schismatic Catholics who deny the pope's authority, it was scandalous for Fr. Martin to receive an award from a group like New Ways Ministry (just as it was scandalous for Pope Francis to meet with Sr. Gramick in October of 2023 and publicly thank her for her ministry).[8]

Fr. Martin's acceptance speech for the New Ways Ministry award was adapted into the 2017 book *Building a Bridge*, and he was also featured in a 2021 documentary by the same title. The documentary includes a scene where Fr. Martin tells attendees at Mass, "I used to say, the Church needs to be welcoming, and that's not enough. That you all, LGBT, need to lead. You need to lead the Church." In another revealing moment, Fr. Martin explains that he doesn't attend

LGBT pride parades because he could get photographed in front of a pro-same-sex "marriage" sign. When the interviewer asks him, "Why would that be such a bad thing?", Fr. Martin replies, "Because I'm not supposed to support same-sex marriage."[9]

Not "I don't support same-sex marriage" or "Because marriage can't be same-sex." Instead, his response is "I'm not supposed to support same-sex marriage," which sounds more like an employee commiserating with a customer about his rigid managers than a spiritual father bearing others' burdens in order to fulfill the law of Christ (Gal. 6:2). I imagine that if the management asked Fr. Martin if he's okay with company policy, he would do his best to give an answer that at least won't get him fired.

Indeed, that's the feeling I get from a 2018 article Fr. Martin wrote in *America* magazine, where he explains what the Church teaches on homosexuality. In one passage, he writes, "All these considerations rule out same-sex marriage. Indeed, official church teaching rules out any sort of sexual activity outside the marriage of a man and a woman."[10]

Robert George is a Catholic philosopher who has done some of the best work defending the Church's teachings on marriage and sexuality. He also calls Fr. Martin a friend despite their disagreements and says that by publishing this article, "Fr. Martin has left no room for detractors (or, for that matter, supporters) to suppose that he believes marriage can be between persons of the same sex or that homosexual conduct can be morally good."[11]

Fr. Martin may not have left room for himself to dissent from Church teaching *at this present moment*, but he has left room for himself to at some point believe that same-sex "marriage" is possible or that homosexual conduct can be morally good.

What Does the Church Say?

Throughout his *America* piece, Fr. Martin says homosexual conduct and same-sex "marriage" are "not approved," "prohibited," and "ruled out." He never says they are sinful, evil, wrong, or immoral. He says the teaching has "some biblical roots" but that it primarily comes from "the traditional interpretation of natural law"—which leaves room for newer interpretations of natural law to supersede those he says are "heavily influenced by the writings of St. Thomas Aquinas." The *Catechism of the Catholic Church* (CCC), on the other hand, says the traditional teaching— that this conduct is gravely depraved—involves "basing itself on Sacred Scripture" (2357), a point Fr. Martin neglects to mention.

This gives the impression that the wrongness of homosexuality lies solely in an ecclesial judgment that can change instead of in the deposit of faith that can't change.

For example, Fr. Martin summarizes what the Church or the *Catechism* teaches but doesn't explicitly say if he agrees with it. He says in the article, "Homosexual acts are, according to the catechism, 'intrinsically disordered.'" But in *Building a Bridge*, Fr. Martin says this term is "needlessly hurtful" when used to describe same-sex attraction. In a 2023 article, Fr. Martin considers it "progress" that "a number of cardinals, archbishops, and bishops have called for the church to reconsider terming homosexual acts as 'intrinsically disordered' in the Catechism."[12]

Another place Fr. Martin has left room for belief in morally good homosexual acts is in the alleged need for a teaching to be "received" by the faithful in order for it to be authoritative. This proposal would allow Fr. Martin to say, "The Church prohibits homosexual conduct" without having to call anyone to repentance who he thinks has not "received" that teaching.

At least, that seems to be the point Fr. Martin is getting at in a 2017 interview with *The Jesuit Post*:

> To take a theological perspective, a teaching must be "received" by the faithful. It's a complex topic (and I am no professional theologian) but, in general, for a teaching to be complete it must be appreciated, accepted, and understood by the faithful. The tradition is that the faithful possess their own inner sense of the authority of a teaching. That's the *sensus fidei* or *sensus fidelium*. You can find out more about it in the Vatican document *Sensus Fidei*. . . . From what many LGBT people tell me, that particular teaching doesn't fit with their own experiences as human beings who love and are loved. So that teaching, it seems, has not been "received" by the LGBT community.[13]

In the introduction to the revised edition of *Building a Bridge*, published in 2018, Fr. Martin briefly alludes to this, saying, "Theologically speaking, you could argue that this teaching has not been 'received' by the LGBT Catholic community, to whom it was primarily directed," though he doesn't elaborate on it not being "complete" because of this fact.[14]

It's beyond the scope of this chapter to fully explain the *sensus fidei*, but it will suffice to say that it means, as the Second Vatican Council taught, that "the entire body of the faithful, anointed as they are by the Holy One, cannot err in matters of belief" (*Lumen Gentium* 12).

However, that doesn't mean every person who says he's Catholic, or even a large number of self-described Catholics, can't err. It may be the case that these so-called faithful actually lack the supernatural gift of faith and are Catholic in name only (like Catholics who attend Church only on Easter out of habit with relatives). The Vatican document

Fr. Martin references says the *sensus fidei* is not identical to public opinion in the Church and that "in the history of the people of God, it has often been not the majority, but rather a minority that has truly lived and witnessed to the Faith" (*Sensus Fidei* 118).

You would think Fr. Martin would be interested in building up the faithful minority, but in 2022, he began to promote *Outreach*, an online magazine that "offer[s] news, essays, resources and community for LGBTQ Catholics, their families and friends, and those who minister to them." But wouldn't you know it? The resources that are offered focus not on things like avoiding near occasions of sin for those who have same-sex attraction, but on undermining the Church's teaching on these issues. These include articles that claim the following:

- The Bible does not condemn LGBT "relationships in any form" and the prohibitions on homosexual conduct in Leviticus "aren't universal moral laws."[15]

- Leviticus says acts of homosexual conduct, bestiality, and child sacrifice are wrong because they "imply imbalanced power dynamics in some way."[16]

- When St. Paul says homosexuality is unnatural, he is just referring to the (false) view that non-human animals don't engage in homosexual behavior.[17]

- "Straight persons" believe that they are "the chosen of God," and the Bible encourages us to include gay persons as also being "chosen of God."[18]

In 2023, *Outreach* hosted a conference with Catholics like Jason Steidl Jack and Fr. Bryan Massingale, who openly dissent against Church teaching, and even non-Catholics like Brandan Robertson who have defended "Christian polyamory."[19] Through publications like *Outreach*, Fr. Martin can put one foot forward in saying, "I have never challenged Church teaching" while taking one step back by allowing dissenters and even non-Catholics to merely "ask questions" that pose a *de facto* challenge to Church teaching.

I call Fr. Martin's habit of saying something that sounds heretical, which he later claims was perfectly orthodox, the "Fr. Martin two-step." Another term for this tactic is the *Motte and Bailey* fallacy.

A Medieval "Bait and Switch"

In 2005, philosopher Nicholas Shackel described an informal fallacy he called the Motte and Bailey doctrine, named after a medieval castle system.[20] In that system, the motte was a heavily defended building or tower that was difficult for an enemy to capture. The bailey, on the other hand, was a wide-open field surrounding the tower that was easy to overtake. But what you give up in security, you gain in livability. The motte was a dark, dank structure in which no one wanted to permanently live. Its only purpose was as a place of refuge in case the more vulnerable bailey was attacked.

According to Shackel, the same thing happens with arguments. A person will occupy the "bailey," or hold a desirable view that is logically weak and therefore easy to refute (like a liberal Catholic who says Pete Buttigieg is "married"). Then, when the bailey is under attack (like when faithful Catholics point out that the Church says these are not marriages), the person will retreat to the less desirable view that is easier to defend—the motte. For Fr. Martin, that is the qualification that Pete Buttigieg is "legally married." Then, once the attackers have given up, the inhabitants will return to the bailey as though nothing had happened. Likewise, critics like Fr. Martin will go back to using the confusing language without any qualifications, since the battle is over, and "what he really meant" will have faded into the past like every other controversy.

Sometimes the practitioners of this strategy will say the "motte" was what they meant the whole time, and the bailey is a "caricature" of their position. In Fr. Martin's case, this happens when he claims that the reason he said "Pete Buttigieg is married" is that the secretary had a marriage registered in City Hall like anyone else. He never meant to say that Buttigieg has a good and natural marriage recognized by canon law or that marriage is simply whatever the State says it is, since those would be indefensible baileys. Instead, he meant only to refer to mundane motte of legal marriage.

In his article "Like it or not, Pete Buttigieg is legally married," Fr. Martin wonders why Catholics become so angry about the idea of Pete and Chasten being married but do not react the same way to other non-Catholic marriages. "When a Jewish couple is married by a rabbi in a synagogue," says Fr. Martin, "most Catholic guests will say, 'Mazel tov!' not 'You're going to burn in hell!'" The only explanation Fr. Martin can come up with is that his critics are upset about their own homosexual attractions and feel threatened by his work.[21] But this response displays a profound ignorance of the Church's teaching on marriage.

God created marriage for the entire human race through the covenant with Adam (i.e., "be fruitful and multiply"). That's why canon law defines marriage (or "the matrimonial covenant") as when "a man and a woman establish between themselves a partnership of the whole of life and which is ordered by its nature to the good of the spouses and the procreation and education of offspring" (*Code of Canon Law* [CIC] 1055).

The *Code* goes on to say that marriage "has been raised by Christ the Lord to the dignity of a sacrament between the baptized." For non-Christians, marriage is still an objective though non-sacramental reality the Church recognizes, which is why those who are divorced and seek remarriage in the Church can do so only if the Church declares their previous marriage null, which is to say they were never married at all.

But two men or two women cannot form a "union" that constitutes a marriage. Of course, that doesn't stop creative critics from saying they can. According to Todd Salzman and Michael Lawler, "both gays and lesbians are naturally sexed human beings and their sexual activity is as incurably infertile as the acts of permanently infertile married hetero-sexuals, which the Catholic Church recognizes as legitimate and ethical."[22]

Sorry: Engaging in acts that have nothing do with procreation and with procreation never resulting has nothing in common with couples engaging in the marital act and procreation never resulting. This kind of reasoning is on par with saying a man flapping his arms is as "incurably grounded" as an eagle with a permanently damaged wing that prevents flight. The man's behavior can't be seriously compared to flight, and the genital stimulation of same-sex couples can't be seriously compared to the marital act. That's why Pope Francis said in *Amoris Laetitia* (The Joy of Love) that "only the exclusive and indissoluble union between a man and a woman has a plenary role to play in society as a stable commitment that bears fruit in new life." He went on to say of same-sex unions that they "may not simply be equated with marriage" (52).

But when Fr. Martin's followers hear him say, "Pete Buttigieg is married," that's exactly the idea they get from him if they don't listen to all the qualifications he gives after he's been chased from the bailey. A 2023 article on *Outreach* makes the same error when its author, a theology professor from Georgetown University, lauds a same-sex couple who will "get married" and muses about how her three elementary school-age children will see "the presence of God" when they attend these (faux) nuptials with her.[23]

When you follow Fr. Martin long enough, you'll find yourself able to predict exactly when he will initiate the "two-step" and retreat to the motte. For example, on October 23, 2019, Fr. Martin tweeted this: "Interesting: 'Where the Bible mentions [same-sex sexual] behavior at all, it clearly condemns it. I freely grant that. The issue is precisely whether the biblical judgment is correct. The Bible sanctioned slavery as well and nowhere attacked it as unjust.'"[24]

When I first saw this tweet, I instantly recognized that Fr. Martin had left himself an escape hatch with the word "interesting." The rest of the tweet after that word was a quote from the Protestant biblical scholar Walter Wink. "I'm just saying it's an interesting view," I envisioned Fr. Martin replying. "Shouldn't we be able to examine views we might not agree with?" And indeed, the next day, Fr. Martin tweeted, "I said that Professor Wink's short article about biblical criticism was 'interesting' (which it was) and was thus lambasted by Catholics who excoriated me for not accepting the 'inerrancy' of Scripture. News flash: Catholics are not biblical fundamentalists."[25]

The same thing happens when Fr. Martin makes statements like "Christians shouldn't do everything that [the] Old Testament commands. Likewise for the Epistles in the New Testament" or when people bring up Levitical prohibitions on homosexuality and Fr. Martin points out that Leviticus also prohibits eating shellfish.[26] When his critics point out the danger of equivocating temporary ceremonial laws with permanent moral laws, Fr. Martin hides in the motte: not every biblical command applies today, so context is key. I mean, do you think it's okay to own slaves even though the Bible regulates slavery?

Once the critics have been satisfied, Fr. Martin's audience wanders out into the bailey of "follow only those biblical commands you agree with."

What's especially irritating about this approach is that Fr. Martin uses it only when a biblical passage condemns a sexual behavior. When Leviticus 18:22 says, "You shall not lie with a male as with a woman; it is an abomination," we are treated to lengthy discussions about context and how not every rule in Leviticus applies today. But when Leviticus 19:34 says, "The alien who resides with you shall be to you as the native-born among you," that simply means the U.S. should have an essentially open borders policy on immigration and not deport those who illegally immigrated. No discussion about "context," or different social environments, or pointing out that the Bible also says we can't eat shellfish is needed. The Bible simply says what it says, and so we should "do according to all for which the foreigner calls to thee" (1 Kings 8:43).[27]

Ultimately, although Fr. Martin may say what sounds like a conservative upholding of Church teaching in *America* magazine, his actions (including his support of a magazine like *Outreach* that undermines Church teaching) say something very different. And his support for Catholic organizations employing people who manifestly persist in grave sins like sodomy (which we will examine in the next chapter) causes even more confusion for the faithful.

2

LGBT
"DISCRIMINATION"

In 2019, Archbishop Charles Thompson ordered Cathedral High School and Brebeuf Jesuit Preparatory School in Indianapolis to sever their relationships with teachers in same-sex "marriages." Cathedral complied, though it seemed to do so out of fear of losing diocesan support more than out of agreement with Catholic teaching.[28] But Brebeuf (which is financially supported by the Jesuits) refused to comply, which led the archbishop to strip the school of its Catholic credentials.

What happened at these schools fits a familiar pattern in the last decade: Catholic schools tolerate teachers in same-sex relationships until diocesan officials finally intervene.

New Ways Ministry claims that over a hundred Catholic school teachers have been removed from their positions because they were in same-sex relationships.[29] Luke Janiki, a self-described gay teacher, writes in *America* magazine that when teachers are removed because of same-sex relationships, "students receive a blunt lesson in what God's justice looks like when no mercy accompanies it. The practice of removing LGBT teachers must end in order for a dialogue to begin."[30] And Fr. Martin says, "The selectivity of focus on LGBT matters when it comes to firings is, to use the words of the Catholic *Catechism*, a 'sign of unjust discrimination' (2358), something we are to avoid."[31]

I agree that firing a teacher merely because he has same-sex attraction could constitute unjust discrimination (especially if the attraction was not publicly disclosed). But firing a teacher for *publicly* flouting Church teaching by engaging in sins like sodomy is an excellent example of just and prudent "discrimination."

Good and Bad Discrimination

Most people have been brought up thinking that "discrimination" is always bad, but what they are thinking of is "unjust discrimination." The *Catechism* uses the word "discrimination" only three times, and in every case, it explicitly or implicitly limits the condemnation to "unjust discrimination."

Discrimination is simply the act of noticing a difference between two things. When a Catholic school doesn't hire someone who is on a sex offender registry, it discriminates between that applicant and a more qualified one (just as your taste buds discriminate between chocolate and sulfur). They recognize a morally relevant difference and act accordingly.

Unjust discrimination, on the other hand, occurs when people are treated differently because of a morally irrelevant trait. Past criminal behavior is morally relevant when it comes to teaching in a school; skin color is not. That's why refusing to hire a sex offender constitutes just discrimination and refusing to hire a black teacher constitutes unjust discrimination.

How does this relate to teachers who identify as LGBT? Sexual behavior is morally relevant to someone's ability to teach in a Catholic school, and it should influence any hiring (or firing) decisions. But notice that I said sexual *behavior* as opposed to sexual *orientation*.

Consider the case of foreign language teacher Michael Griffin, who was fired in 2013 from Holy Ghost Preparatory High School in Pennsylvania. Apparently, Griffin announced in an email to administrators that he was going to be late to school because he was on his way to file for a license to marry his boyfriend. *The Huffington Post* said, "Griffin was fired essentially for being gay" and lists the story under the topic "fired for being gay."[32]

But Griffin wasn't fired for "being gay."

It would be one thing if a school fired a teacher because he attended a Catholic support group for people who experience same-sex attraction but uphold the Church's teaching on chastity. That could be a case of firing someone merely "for being gay," and people could legitimately raise the issue of whether such a move is prudent. But Griffin was fired not because of a private disposition, but because he chose to publicly violate Church teaching by trying to marry another man.

The First Amendment prevents the government from prohibiting the "free exercise of religion," and one of those exercises is a religion's ability to select its own ministers. Because of what is called "the ministerial exception," radical feminists can't sue the Catholic Church for the right to have the "job" of being a priest. And this exception applies not only to ordained clergy like priests, since many religions also have "teaching ministers" like pastors, rabbis, and teachers in religious schools.

In 2012, the U.S. Supreme Court unanimously decided in *Hosanna-Tabor Evangelical Lutheran Church and School v. Equal Employment Opportunity Commission* that the ministerial exception applies to teachers in religious schools, even if they teach a nonreligious subject like math. Several dioceses have required teachers to sign contracts stating that they are "ministers of the gospel" because they are role models and often share personal views with students on non-academic subjects. In 2020, the Supreme Court reaffirmed *Hosanna-Tabor* in *Our Lady of Guadalupe School v. Morrissey-Berru*, saying the ministerial exception applies to positions that lack the formal title of "minister." Fr. Matt Malone, the editor of *America* magazine, opined that the ministerial exception is correct but also said churches

> should not exercise that freedom in pursuit of an indiscriminate purging of church employees simply because they hold unorthodox views or have made life choices that do not accord with Catholic teaching. That would be wrong and would be a source of grave scandal for the faithful and for the country we seek to evangelize."[33]

But Fr. Malone doesn't really believe that a person's "life choices" should have *no impact* on his employment at a church or school. He may say this for LGBT employees, but in other obvious cases of unsuitable employees, I'm sure he'd demand their dismissal, which raises a larger question: what "life choices" make someone unfit to be a Catholic school teacher?

Wanted: "Genuinely" Catholic Teachers

Fr. Martin agrees that "church organizations have the authority to require their employees to follow church teachings." But he claims that LGBT employees are singled out for their behavior, whereas "straight" employees can engage in all kinds of indiscretions without fear of being fired. He complains that this standard isn't applied to divorced Catholics in extramarital relationships and people who use contraception. He even goes further and says, "To be consistent, shouldn't we fire people for not helping the poor, for not being forgiving, or for not being loving? For being cruel?"[34]

In some cases, yes!

A cruel teacher who verbally, physically, emotionally, or in any other way abuses his students should be terminated immediately. Same with a teacher who "unlovingly" allows his classrooms to be a free-for-all or even is chronically late to school. Even outside the classroom, employees caught in a viral video abusing a service worker, and thus bringing scandal upon the school they work at, will quickly find themselves out of a job.

We have a principle to sort out which teachers should be fired: does the behavior hinder the person's ability to carry out his job? In order to answer that question, we must answer this question: what is the job of a Catholic school teacher or faculty member?

It's not to merely teach a subject at a Catholic school. Some people think religious instruction is only the responsibility of the theology department. But every employee of a Catholic school has a responsibility to strengthen the faith of Catholic students and evangelize non-Catholic students. The *National Directory for Catechesis*, published by the USCCB, states, "All teachers in Catholic schools share in the catechetical ministry. 'All members of the faculty, at least by their example, are an integral part of the process of religious education. . . . Teachers' lifestyle and character are as important as their professional credentials'" (233).

Even teachers of secular subjects share in catechesis through the example their personal conduct sets. They talk about news and current events before official classroom instruction begins. They form friendships with students, who end up learning about their personal lives. Students look up to them as role models. That's why, if these teachers are *bad* Catholic role models, they should be let go. Schools aren't demanding that teachers be perfect—just that they not be perverts.

What about teachers in invalid marriages or ones who use contraception? If they boast about these sins to students, then they should be treated like LGBT teachers who boast about sins like sodomy or contracting a counterfeit marriage. But just because these private sins are usually not discovered, that does not mean schools should refrain from firing teachers who cause scandal through publicly grave acts. During his 2004 visit to the United States, Pope John Paul II said,

> It is of utmost importance, therefore, that the Church's institutions be genuinely Catholic: Catholic in their self-understanding and Catholic in their identity. All those who share in the apostolates of such institutions, including those who are not of the Faith, should show a sincere and respectful appreciation of that mission that is their inspiration and ultimate *raison d'être.*[35]

Other moral faults don't hinder a teacher's ability to carry out the school's mission. It is sinful never to help the poor, but this sort of perpetual stinginess doesn't impact a teacher's ability to teach students, provided that he doesn't publicly undermine the Church's teachings on poverty by doing something like publicly defending *social Darwinism*, which claims that we should let the poor "die off."

So now we have a workable standard: people who engage in *public, grave sins* are unfit to be Catholic school teachers because they scandalize students and undermine Church teaching. Schools don't need to scrutinize tax returns to see if teachers are donating enough to charity. But they can fire a teacher who openly advocates for eugenics and social Darwinism in order to get rid of poor people.

Some teachers in real marriages (as opposed to same-sex pairings being called marriages) may themselves engage in sodomy or masturbation, but those private sins would not merit dismissal unless they were publicly disclosed (like in a sex education class gone awry). Same-sex couples who brag about their "marriages" are practically wearing a neon sign saying they engage in grave evils like sodomy, and so the cases are completely different.

Even people who publicly *advocate* for grave evils are unfit to be Catholic school teachers, as was the case with a Maryland teacher who was fired for writing posts at a white supremacist website, and a teacher in South Carolina who was fired for expressing support on social media for legal abortion.[36]

Can you imagine Fr. Martin offering his typical logic in these cases? "If you fire someone for being racist, you have to fire every teacher who's unloving. This is discrimination!" Of course not, because whereas Fr. Martin believes that all acts of racism are wicked, he doesn't believe that sodomy is wicked. (I will eat this page of my book if he corrects me and is willing to publicly say, "All sexual acts between people of the same sex are wicked.") But if distorting the value of the human person through racism is enough to make someone unfit to teach in a Catholic school, then why wouldn't distorting our sexuality?

Do Teachers Have to Be Catholic?

Fr. Martin's favorite example of Catholic school employees whom we shouldn't expect to live under Church teachings is non-Catholics. In *Building a Bridge*, he asks if Catholic organizations should fire Protestants, Unitarians, Jews, and atheists. He says Catholic organizations don't do this because "we are selective—perhaps unconsciously, perhaps consciously—about which church teachings matter."[37]

Catholic school administrators shouldn't fire someone because of the religion he practiced when he was hired. But if teachers are lay ministers of the Faith, then yes—you should hire and fire teachers based on their religious affiliation. For example, if a teacher was Catholic when he was hired but later left the Faith and is now publicly espousing atheism on social media, he should be shown the door. Even faculty who aren't on social media end up sharing their personal views on religious matters with students, so their decision to reject the Catholic faith justifies the school rejecting them in favor of a more faithful employee.

That's why the Church's *Code of Canon Law* says, "Formation and education in a Catholic school must be based on the principles of Catholic doctrine, and the teachers must be outstanding in true doctrine and uprightness of life" (803.2). The *National Directory for Catechesis* advises Catholic school leaders to "recruit teachers who are practicing Catholics, who can understand and accept the teachings of the Catholic Church and the moral demands of the gospel and who can contribute to the achievement of the school's Catholic identity and apostolic goals."

The *Directory* does acknowledge that although "some situations might entail compelling reasons for members of another faith tradition to teach in a Catholic school, as much as possible, all teachers in a Catholic school should be practicing Catholics" (233). For example, if there are no applications from Catholic math teachers, then you may hire a Protestant who is willing to promote the Catholic faith and in no way publicly oppose its teachings.

But given that less than one percent of U.S. households include same-sex couples, it shouldn't be difficult to find an applicant who at least satisfies *that* aspect of Catholic teaching.[38] Also, hiring a non-Catholic teacher doesn't affirm a fundamental error in society about something as important as the institution of marriage. Employing a teacher in a same-sex "marriage" is not like hiring an Anglican; it's like hiring an abortionist.

When you come across Catholics who cry, "Discrimination!" at these episodes, seek agreement about administrators' right to fire teachers who can't carry out their jobs. Then focus on the question, "What is a Catholic school teacher's fundamental job?" Hopefully, you will get them to see that it is to form students' minds and hearts to love and serve God, and teachers who publicly reject basic teachings regarding faith or morals are simply unfit to be teachers within a Catholic school.

3

LGBT PRIDE FLAGS

In 2022, Bishop Robert McManus of Worcester, Massachusetts stripped a Jesuit middle school of its Catholic status after it refused to stop flying an LGBT pride flag and a Black Lives Matter flag on campus. McManus said this contradicted a letter he wrote in May, which said, "These symbols [flags] embody specific agendas or ideologies [that] contradict Catholic social and moral teaching." He said the Church "stands unequivocally behind the phrase 'black lives matter'" but that BLM "promotes a platform that directly contradicts Catholic social teaching" (a point we'll return to in chapter fourteen).

With regard to the LGBT rainbow "pride flag," McManus said it "represents support of gay marriage and actively living a LGBTQ+ lifestyle," and "The flying of these flags in front of a Catholic school sends a mixed, confusing, and scandalous message to the public about the Church's stance on these important moral and social issues."[39] But not to many liberal Catholics, who say, as the school's principal did, that the flags merely "state that all are welcome at [the school] and this value of inclusion is rooted in Catholic teaching."

The *National Catholic Reporter* published five letters to the editor on the story, all of them denouncing the bishop, including one that said, "With activities like those of McManus, the church in the U.S. needs little additional help in emptying out its churches."[40] Fr. James Martin defended Catholics celebrating "pride month" because, according to him, "Pride Month is mainly about supporting the fundamental human rights of the LGBTQ community: the right to live in safety, the right to be treated as equals, and the right to be fully welcome in society."[41]

But this doesn't justify Catholics promoting a symbol that is directly opposed to the teachings of their faith.

Tolerance Then, Celebration Now

The LGBT pride flag represents more than the "fundamental human rights," like the right to life, of those who identify as LGBT. Indeed, for many people who fly the pride flag, those "fundamental rights" include the right to "marry" people of the same sex, which the Catholic Church opposes. The Church doesn't just oppose Catholics engaging in same-sex "marriages"; it opposes society's attempts to redefine something God created for humanity. The State can no more validly redefine marriage than it can redefine "womanhood" or "humanity" (though it certainly tries). This design is so deeply engrained into human nature that it makes same-sex "marriage" as impossible as a square circle.

Fr. Martin claims that "pride month" is about recognizing an LGBT person's right to live in societies and opposition to cultures that treat homosexuality as a capital offense. But we already have a word for recognizing a person's right to live, even if you strongly denounce his moral choices:

tolerance. A person can tolerate aberrant sexual behavior (that doesn't threaten the common good), but he definitely shouldn't be proud of it.

And of course, tolerance was never the end goal of the LGBT movement.

Arguing for "tolerance" was a necessary concession (a toleration, if you will) during the 1990s, when most people opposed homosexual behavior. The strategy changed once the LGBT movement made enough cultural headway to demand not just toleration of disordered behavior, but *celebration* of it. Now it is the LGBT advocates who refuse to tolerate Christians. For example, when five players of the Tampa Bay Rays refused to wear a rainbow logo on their uniforms at an event in 2022, they said it was because, as pitcher Jason Adam put it,

> a lot of guys decided that it's just a lifestyle that maybe—
> not that they look down on anybody or think differently—
> it's just that maybe we don't want to encourage it if we
> believe in Jesus, who's encouraged us to live a lifestyle
> that would abstain from that behavior, just like [Jesus]
> encourages me as a heterosexual male to abstain from sex
> outside of the confines of marriage.[42]

Notice that Adam and the other players weren't condemning this behavior. They just said they don't want to encourage it. But in spite of this meek reply, many commenters savaged the team's decision to let them play, with one saying the Rays were "allowing homophobia among a handful of twenty-somethings."[43] When Philadelphia Flyers hockey player Ivan Provorov refused to wear a rainbow jersey for a 2023 "pride night," NHL analyst E.J. Hradek said Povorov should "get on a plane" to his home country of Russia and fight against Ukraine. (Can you imagine what would happen if a Christian analyst told a Muslim player to "go back" to his home country?)[44]

The pride flag is intimately connected to the LGBT activist movement and its goal of purging society of any negative attitudes toward LGBT identities and behaviors. The flag was the creation of a self-identified gay man named Gilbert Baker, who grew up in 1960s San Francisco. The first color on the original rainbow flag was hot pink and symbolized sexuality (though the color was dropped because the fabric was expensive).

In 2021, the Ottawa Catholic School Board in Canada voted to permanently fly the rainbow flag at its schools. Unlike in the U.S., the Canadian government directly funds its country's Catholic schools. The bishops set catechetical curricula, but local decisions are overseen by trustees elected to school boards. This means that instead of the bishops running Catholic schools, you get people whose credentials are that they "went to Catholic school for twelve years," and they give the game away about the flag being more than just a reference to "human dignity." According to an article in the *Ottawa Citizen*,

> trustee Spencer Warren, who moved the motion, said it is something he has been passionate about since being a trustee with the Ottawa Catholic School Board. "[I] believe that everyone has the right to be loved unconditionally and be treated with dignity. After all, Love is Love!" Warren wrote in an email.[45]

A Confederate Counterexample

According to liberal Catholics, there is nothing wrong with flying or sharing the rainbow flag because, *according to them*, the flag symbolizes only a group of people with sexual orientations. Those who fly the flag get to determine its meaning, and so they have the authority to say it promotes only innocuous messages like "LGBT people are welcome here." But these critics won't allow that same explanation for flags they consider morally offensive.

In 2015, the *National Catholic Reporter* ran a story about a young activist who tore down a state courthouse's Confederate flag and noted that the flag "represents for many a war to uphold slavery and, later, a battle to oppose civil rights advances."[46] After the death of George Floyd in 2020, a Catholic school and church in Alabama removed images of the Confederate flag.[47] One contributor in *America* magazine recalls how when he was a youth, his high school in southern Detroit would wave a Confederate flag at football games when its team competed against their rivals in northern Detroit. He writes,

> What were all these wealthy white kids doing waving a Confederate flag? We, who boasted one of the best public school systems in the country—including an innovative American studies curriculum—what the hell were we thinking? What message did we send to the opposing teams and communities, some of which were more diverse than ours? And what kind of damage did we inflict on others and ourselves?[48]

Notice in all these examples that it doesn't matter if those flying the Confederate flag personally consider it a symbol of Southern culture and it has no racial animus for them. What *they* think about the flag doesn't matter. All that matters is that some people have associated the flag with evil, and that means anyone who flies it is guilty of promoting those evil views.

In their 2018 pastoral letter *Open Wide Our Hearts*, the U.S. bishops speak about racist symbols and say, "The reappearance of symbols of hatred, such as nooses and swastikas in public spaces, is a tragic indicator of rising racial and ethnic animus."[49] In response, Catholic activist and religion professor Eric Martin penned an article for *Sojourners* about the statement entitled "The Catholic Church Has a Visible White-Power Faction." Martin's article was temporarily removed because it erroneously stated that the bishops were silent on the swastika, the noose, and the Confederate flag.

Unlike the swastika and the noose, the final draft of *Open Wide Our Hearts* made no mention of the Confederate flag. However, the bishops did explain in a statement before the document's release that "while for many the Confederate flag is also a sign of hatred and segregation, some still claim it as a sign of heritage." Martin quoted only the latter half of this statement about the "heritage" of the flag before issuing a biting rebuttal: "this logic indefensibly hand-waves the history of slavery, murderous opposition to civil rights, and violence such as the 2015 shooting at a black church in Charleston, S.C., as a vaguely benign 'heritage.'"[50]

Another example would be liberal contempt for red "Make America Great Again" (MAGA) baseball caps, made popular by President Donald Trump. In a 2019 article for *Commonweal*, Mollie Wilson O'Reilly said that wearing a MAGA hat was the equivalent of "suiting up for Team Racist." She called Catholics to reject the symbol wholesale and said, "If you welcome some of what President Trump has done but abhor his racism, it's up to you to figure out how to express those convictions. Wearing MAGA gear says you're not bothered."[51]

But imagine if I told Mollie Wilson O'Reilly that "wearing a MAGA hat doesn't mean I support every Trump policy or every person who votes for Trump." Her response would probably be that my scandalous choice of garb says more than any "after-the-fact" explanation could. And the O'Reillys of the world should have the same response for people like Fr. James Martin, who claim that "just because you celebrate Pride Month doesn't mean that you necessarily agree with what every person, every organization, or even every float in every parade has to say."[52]

Sorry, but you can't have it both ways. If people like O'Reilly or Fr. Martin say it's wrong to fly a Confederate flag, or even wear a "MAGA" hat, just because *some* people use these symbols in service of evils like racism, then from their own logic, it would be just as wrong to fly a pride flag because some people use it in promotion of evils like sodomy.

Appropriate Solidarity?

Some Catholics say it is appropriate to wear, fly, or share the pride flag if it is done to show solidarity with victims of violence who identify as LGBT. For example, after the 2016 shooting at a gay nightclub called Pulse in Orlando, Florida that killed forty-nine people, Fr. Martin criticized bishops who condemned the violence without speaking about it being motivated by homophobia. However, later evidence showed that the attacker was LGBT himself and acted out of revenge for U.S. military strikes in the Middle East. The attacker originally targeted a Disney World attraction before he switched to a target with less security.[53]

We should always show solidarity and support with innocent victims of violence, but before Christians associate themselves with any particular symbol to accomplish that task, they have to assess the morality of the symbol itself. Nothing, not even compassion for the victimized, can justify promoting a message that is at odds with the gospel.

Would an act of violence against a group of Satanists make it appropriate to put their version of the pentagram on our social media profiles? No! Even though it would be wrong to violently attack Satanists who aren't in the process of directly harming someone, there are other ways to show support for these victims without promoting a symbol associated with demons and blasphemy.

That's why the Archdiocese of Toronto dedicated the month of June not to celebrating LGBT pride, but to the Sacred Heart of Jesus. When the Toronto Catholic school board voted to fly rainbow flags at its schools, the archdiocese released a statement saying that a more appropriate symbol of inclusion and love to promote at a Catholic school is the cross of Christ: "The cross outside of Catholic schools and any Catholic church, hospital, or institution signals our commitment that all who enter the building are welcomed and loved in their beauty and uniqueness as children of God."

4

THE SIN OF SCANDAL

In June of 2017, Bishop Thomas Paprocki of Springfield, Illinois issued a decree forbidding persons in same-sex "marriages" from receiving Communion or from being received into the Church if they choose not to end their relationships. Pastors were instructed to meet with such individuals in private and call them to conversion through the sacrament of reconciliation. The decree also said that those who died without repenting of being in these relationships were to be withheld funeral rites. Some of the more histrionic responses made it sound as though Paprocki had told churches to unceremoniously throw the bodies of LGBT people into unmarked graves.

The president of Dignity USA said, "This document is mean-spirited and hurtful in the extreme," while New Ways Ministry said the bishop's promise to punish those who violate his directive "borders on spiritual abuse."[54] Fr. James Martin, on the other hand, merely chose to retweet a piece from the *National Catholic Reporter* with the headline "The scandal may be in not holding funerals for gay spouses, theologians say"—which implies that the real scandal is the bishop's original directive.

This same argument is used to criticize bishops who prohibit Catholics who identify as LGBT from serving on parish councils or in liturgical functions like being a lector or choir member. And though these cases aren't as emotionally fraught as funerals, they all involve a similar application of the Church's teaching on scandal. As such, we'll use the context of funerals to investigate the teaching, because if it can be applied in an emotionally difficult case, then it will apply in less emotional cases like lay ministries.

Stumbling over Scandal

One reason funerals can involve scandal is because of the temptation to turn them into miniature canonization sessions. Given the grief of the deceased's loved ones, it's understandable that they may find comfort in talking about their loved one already being in heaven. But the primary purpose of Catholic funerals is to pray for the deceased because we do not absolutely know if they died in a state of grace. Or, if they did, we do not know how much purification they need before they are able to enter into heaven (CCC 1030-1031).

That's why the *General Instruction of the Roman Missal* says, "At the Funeral Mass there should, as a rule, be a short homily, but never a eulogy of any kind" (382). The late Cincinnati archbishop Daniel Pilarczyk once put it this way: "The funeral liturgy is a celebration of salvation and mercy, of grace and eternal life. It is not meant to be a commemoration (much less a canonization) of the person who has died. Extended remembering of the deceased often results in forgetting the Lord."[55]

Along with serving the deceased through our prayers for them, a Christian funeral can inspire those who have separated themselves from God through mortal sin to reconcile with God as soon as possible. The presence of the deceased tells them, *Memento mori*: remember that you will die, too! But if people see the hope of salvation being discussed in the context of someone who never repented of a grave sin like sodomy, adultery, robbery, or murder, then they may come to the erroneous conclusion that even if the Church says these behaviors are sinful, they can't be *so* sinful as to risk anyone's salvation.

But in an editorial in the *National Catholic Reporter*, Todd Salzman and Michael Lawler take issue with the idea that funerals for couples in same-sex "marriages" would result in scandal:

> Wherein lies the scandal in the case under discussion? Is it in permitting a church funeral to a deceased same-sex partner that would lead others to engage in homosexual behavior, or is it in the behavior of the bishops directing priests to deny a church funeral to a deceased spouse in a same-sex marriage that would lead others to engage in discriminatory attitudes and behaviors toward same-sex couples in specific, or members of the LGBT community in general?[56]

Salzman and Lawler say the greater harm is the possible "scandal" that people will think the Church discriminates against people who identify as LGBT. According to them, a morally wrong behavior like sodomy "is not always morally bad if it is done with a good attitude."

The authors reach this startling conclusion by noting that the *Catechism* defines scandal as "an attitude or behavior which leads another to do evil" (2284). They claim that attitudes are either always good (promoting justice) or always bad (seeking vainglory). They then say that, depending on the attitude, as well as a well-informed conscience, a wrong behavior may not be morally bad and may even be morally good. If the behavior is not morally bad, it follows that there is no grave sin and, therefore, no legitimate public scandal.

An *Amoris Laetitia* Loophole

Salzman and Lawler cite an observation in Pope Francis's 2016 apostolic exhortation *Amoris Laeitita*: that some people in invalid marriages may not fully consent to the sexual act. For example, a woman who worries about her "husband"— that is, the man with whom she's cohabiting—abandoning her and her children and leaving them without a means to survive in a country that lacks social services might acquiesce to sexual relations (adultery) and not be culpable for a grave sin. But Salzman and Lawler take this reasoning and turn it into a sweeping exemption for all sexual immorality:

> Factors may exist in *all irregular situations* [emphasis added] which limit "deliberate consent" and the ability to make a fully informed moral decision (*Amoris Laetitia* 301). If deliberate consent is lacking or somehow diminished, there can be no grave sin and, therefore, no scandal in permitting a church funeral to a deceased same-sex partner.

This mentality would paralyze our moral judgments and render the concept of scandal useless. If it were applied consistently, then *no evil act could ever be scandalous* because lessened culpability is possible in all sins, sexual or not.

A similar relativism can be seen in Bonnette's article that I cited in chapter one about attending a same-sex "wedding." She says, "As a straight woman, I do not need to form my conscience around what is good with regard to LGBTQ persons. That is between them and God."[57] Would Bonnette apply the same logic to polygamists? What about racists or employers who mistreat their workers? Would she say, "As a non-business owner, I do not need to form my conscience around what is good with regard to business owners"?

We may not be able to judge a person's invisible soul, but we can judge the person's visible actions, and so we should never give the impression that intrinsically evil *acts* could be morally good. In *Veritatis Splendor* (The Splendor of Truth), Pope John Paul II said,

> The negative moral precepts, those prohibiting certain concrete actions or kinds of behavior as intrinsically evil, do not allow for any legitimate exception. They do not leave room, in any morally acceptable way, for the "creativity" of any contrary determination whatsoever. Once the moral species of an action prohibited by a universal rule is concretely recognized, the only morally good act is that of obeying the moral law and of refraining from the action which it forbids (67).

Amoris Laetitia even warns against interpretations that would generalize a willful neglect of the moral law:

> A lukewarm attitude, any kind of relativism, or an undue reticence in proposing that ideal, would be a lack of fidelity to the gospel and also of love on the part of the Church for young people themselves. To show understanding in the face of exceptional situations never implies dimming the light of the fuller ideal, or proposing less than what Jesus offers to the human being (307).

Salzman and Lawler are also incorrect when they say the prohibition on funerals for unrepentant same-sex couples is because the Church has moral certainty that the person died in a state of grave sin. Concern about scandal relates to the Church implicitly communicating that certain *acts* like sodomy and adultery do not mortally wound our souls.

In response, they claim it is "hard to imagine" that allowing these funerals will cause people to think Church teaching has changed on homosexual conduct. People already know what the Church teaches on the matter, so why risk causing people to think the Church has an unloving stance toward LGBT people? But by that logic, why should the Church prohibit any scandalous funerals?

In 2002, the Diocese of Brooklyn denied a Mass for the murderous crime lord John Gotti but permitted him to be buried next to his son in a Catholic cemetery.[58] In 2015, a diocese in Italy was lambasted for allowing a lavish funeral for mob boss Vittorio Casamonica, which had come to be used as "Mafia propaganda."[59] But why is that scandalous? After all, it's "hard to imagine" that such a funeral would make people think the Church's teaching on murder and extortion had now changed.

The answer is that funerals are associated with a reasonable hope of heaven for the deceased. To celebrate one for those who die without repenting from public, grave sin dulls our consciences toward the *gravity* of those sins, even if we intellectually still place the activity in the "sin" category.

Casamonica's funeral became lavish propaganda for one kind of evil; the same can easily happen at funerals for people who spent their lives unrepentantly celebrating sins and disorders related to sexuality. In 2024, St. Patrick's Cathedral in New York hosted a packed funeral for atheistic transgender activist Cecilia Gentili, at which provocatively dressed attendees praised the deceased as "St. Cecilia, mother of all whores" and danced in the aisles. The archdiocese, which did not have advance knowledge about Gentili's atheistic, transgender identity, later offered a Mass of reparation in response to the sacrilege and scandal related to the service.[60]

That's why what Pope Francis said about the Mafia would also apply to Catholics engaged in other grave sins: "The Lord is waiting for you, and the Church will welcome you if your willingness to serve good is as clear and public as your choice to serve evil was."[61]

Salzman's and Lawler's other argument is that such a prohibition will encourage Catholics to engage in truly unjust discrimination against same-sex couples, though the duo present no evidence of this. And by this logic, the authors would have to say actions like taking food from an abandoned store during a disaster (which is morally licit if done out of necessity) are "scandalous." After all, couldn't it lead people into thinking petty theft is moral? Whereas it is sinful to reject the Church's teachings, it is not scandalous for the Church to preach truths that our culture rejects. Indeed, our Lord's preaching resulted in some disciples no longer following him (John 6:66), and St. Paul says, "We preach Christ crucified, a stumbling block (*skandalon*) to Jews and folly to Gentiles" (1 Cor. 1:23).

All Manifest Sinners?

According to the *Code of Canon Law*, "deceased members of the Christian faithful must be given ecclesiastical funerals according to the norm of law" (1176.1). This also includes catechumens who die before they receive the sacraments of initiation, like baptism and confirmation (1183.1). If a bishop deems it appropriate, a funeral can also be given to children who died before being baptized or even, in some cases, to a baptized non-Catholic (1183.2-3). The inclusion of catechumens and unbaptized children shows that the Church wants to provide funerals for as many believers as possible, and burying the dead itself is a corporal work of mercy (CCC 2300).

However, canon 1184 stipulates that

unless [the deceased] gave some signs of repentance be-fore death, the following must be deprived of ecclesiasti-cal funerals:

- notorious apostates, heretics, and schismatics;
- those who chose the cremation of their bodies for reasons contrary to Christian faith; and
- other manifest sinners who cannot be granted ecclesiastical funerals without public scandal of the faithful.

New Ways Ministry member Robert Shine published an editorial criticizing Bishop Paprocki's decree, saying it is discriminatory to apply canon 1184 to those in same-sex "marriages" because in one sense, we are all "manifest sinners." He writes,

It is discrimination to target LGBT people when, in a cer-tain sense, all Catholics could be deemed "manifest sinners." Who among us, including Bishop Paprocki, does not public-ly sin at different moments? Yet, funeral rites are not denied to Catholics who pay employees an unjust wage, publicly advocate for the death penalty, or deny climate change.[62]

I'll talk about climate change in chapter fifteen, but for now I'll say you don't have to go to confession if you don't accept certain scientific theories related to climate change. You don't even have to go to confession if you think the sun orbits the earth (i.e., *geocentrism*). The Church binds the faithful to believe only matters related to faith and morals, which excludes purely scientific hypotheses.

More importantly, Shine's definition of "manifest sin" as any sin that has been "manifested" or has become publicly known is laughable. Public knowledge of a sin doesn't change its gravity. A person could be widely known for making a rude comment on social media, but he wouldn't be a "manifest sinner." In contrast, a person who secretly looks at pornography would be gravely sinning even if his behavior is never made manifest.

Shine's interpretation of a "manifest sinner" would either lead to no one being given an ecclesiastical funeral or, more likely, to a moral indifferentism that says we're all "manifest sinners," so we shouldn't call anyone to repentance. The *New Commentary on the Code of Canon Law* provides a far better definition when it says a person is in "manifest sin" when he is "publicly known to be living in a state of grave sin."[63]

That means that manifest sin doesn't occur merely because one's impulsive bad behavior got caught in a viral video. Manifest sin, rather, involves someone both habitually living in a state of grave sin and doing so in a way that publicly announces his situation to the world. Notorious gangsters like John Gotti and Paul Castellano were denied Catholic funerals because of their persistence in manifest sin until death. A socialite who proudly cavorts with his mistress at public events or two men who publicly announce to the world that they are in a sexual relationship by contracting a same-sex "marriage" would also fit this definition.

Just Another "Invalid" Marriage

Fr. Martin claims that if people in same-sex "marriages" should be denied Catholic funerals, then the same standard should be applied to cohabiting couples and people whose marriages were invalid and not reconciled with the

Church prior to death. But there is a legitimate question about how much the sins in these relationships have been "publicly manifested."

In almost every case, the appearance and names of the people in a same-sex "marriage" clearly signify the disordered nature of the relationship. This is not just another invalid marriage; it is a relationship *pretending* to be a marriage that can never become one. Two women in such a situation might engage in sexual behavior, but they can never experience matrimony because they can't engage in the sexual act ordered toward procreation. The Latin roots of *matrimony* even mean "mother's obligation," and two women cannot make themselves mothers together. Also, given the unique political climate surrounding the issue of homosexuality, such a funeral could attract widespread attention and be used as a platform to misinform people about the Church's teachings or as a rallying cry to change those teachings and undermine the Church's authority.

In an invalid marriage, only those who had personal knowledge of the situation would know about the irregularity, and so the potential for scandal is much lower, because the person's sin was not "publicly manifested." That doesn't mean there is *no* potential for scandal; some theologians insist that funerals for Catholics in invalid marriages are scandalous, and so they should not be celebrated. The Diocese of Bridgeport, Connecticut, for example, allows funeral Masses for Catholics in invalid marriages who upheld Church teaching (by living as brother and sister, for example) but recommends the "Funeral Liturgy Outside Mass" for those who neglected the Church's teaching on marriage in this regard.[64]

Even though critics like Fr. Martin deny this, it is possible to be compassionate toward those who suffer without scandalizing others and leading them into sin.

A pastor or parish staff member faced with a request for a church funeral for a same-sex "spouse" should remember that the surviving member of such a couple will certainly be experiencing sorrowful grief. He may also be suffering from loneliness, depression, or financial hardship. Catholics should reach out to such a person, who is created in the image of God and loved by him, and strive to meet his basic human needs through empathy and acts of charity, especially to help alleviate the financial burdens and emotional toll that accompany burying a loved one.

This person may be hurt by the denial of a Catholic funeral, but if Catholics offer compassion, this person can have a genuine encounter with Christ, who always calls us to conversion and gives us the grace to follow him in any circumstance.

5

TRANSGENDER IDEOLOGY

In 2022, the Archdiocese of Milwaukee released a policy on how to treat individuals who identify as transgender. An article in the *National Catholic Reporter* said it "takes aim at transpersons," and a priest in Chicago called it "a callous, anti-intellectual, and anti-human dumpster fire of a document unworthy of any association with the name of our Lord and brother."[65]

Those are strange words for a document that said gender dysphoria "is not sinful in itself but rather reflects the broader disharmony caused by original sin" and "such persons should be treated with respect and with charity, and no one should suffer bullying, violence, insults, or unjust discrimination based on such experiences."[66] The policy went on to, among other things, prohibit the use of "preferred pronouns," insist that people use locker rooms in accord with their biological sex, and prohibit "puberty-blockers" from being administered on Church grounds.

All of this would have been considered innocuous ten years ago, but now some liberal Catholics caught up in the cultural zeitgeist insist that the Church must embrace transgender ideology. This includes not just wayward laity and priests, but even entire bishops' conferences.

The "Science" of Sex

On March 12, 2023, the German synodal way passed an implementation text entitled "Dealing with Gender Diversity," with 96 percent approval from synodal delegates and a majority of German bishops supporting it. According to the Catholic News Agency, the document urged support for "changing baptism records to match someone's self-identified gender, banning one's gender identity from consideration for pastoral ministerial roles," and mandatory education for priests and church employees to "deal with the topic of gender diversity."

The statement said Catholics should affirm transgender identities because, though it recognizes biological sex, determined primarily by chromosomes, it also says that sex "can by no means be reduced to this. Instead, the biological gender identity develops in complicated interactions between genetic and epigenetic factors and is above all decisively shaped by the 'hormonal sex.'"[67]

It then discusses the sexually ambiguous organs and appearances that can occur in people who are *intersex*, or have both male and female sex organs. But this conflates extremely rare intersex conditions (one out of 2,000 births) with transgender identity and makes it seem as though there's no objective way to determine if someone is a man or a woman. However, in almost all cases of transgender identities, a person's genes, skeleton, and hormones all correspond to the same sex—the person simply has an incorrect sense of his own identity.

"Dealing with Gender Diversity" also refuses to accept that a person could be mistaken about his sexual identity. In fact, for all its talk of inclusion, nowhere does the statement mention how the Church should help those who *detransition*, or go back to accepting their true sex even after engaging in medical mutilation falsely called "gender reassignment treatments." These are people who need the Church the most because they are often shunned by the transgender community as "traitors." They also feel out of place among people of their own sex because of the effects of surgery or cross-sex hormones on their bodies. The Church should be a place where everyone feels welcome and encouraged to seek holiness, no matter what unfortunate choices they made in the past.

The statement also says previous Vatican teaching on transgender identities and intersex conditions "is characterized by an understanding of these terms that corresponds neither to the self-understanding of the people concerned nor to the state of the human sciences." Other liberal Catholics say the Church simply hasn't caught up with "the science" on transgender ideology. Fr. Bryan Massingale, an openly gay priest who teaches moral theology at Fordham, says, "The hierarchy has had comparatively little time to absorb and reflect upon the findings in the human sciences about the complexity of gender and sexuality."[68] Fr. Daniel Horan, a professor at the all-female St. Mary's College, even penned an article entitled "Recent transphobic statements from bishops make truth claims without facts."[69]

And just what are these "scientific facts" that overturn what we've known about men and women for thousands of years? Fr. Horan and Fr. Massingale don't say in their articles, but the general tack liberal Catholics take is to appeal to things like brain scan studies that show that a transgender person's brain resembles those of the opposite sex with which he identifies. These bits of apparent scientific evidence embolden liberal Catholics to conclude that a person may not belong to the sex he was "assigned at birth."

First, sex isn't *assigned* at birth as if it were a role in a company. It is *discovered* at birth, and even before birth through blood tests and ultrasounds. True, there are cases involving ambiguous genitalia or anomalous chromosomes, where we may not be sure at first if someone is a man or woman (i.e., intersex cases), but these don't prevent doctors from determining the person's sex after enough tests are performed.

Even if there were a handful of hard cases where we weren't sure if an individual was male or female, that wouldn't disprove the sexual binary everyone else belongs to, just as the rare case of a chicken living for 18 months with his head cut off (look up "Mike the Headless Chicken" if you aren't squeamish) doesn't disprove the fact that life and death are, almost always, easily confirmed, "binary" realities.

Second, these "brain scan" arguments prove only that people who have identity disorders may also have brain abnormalities. It doesn't prove that they really belong to the other sex. For example, people with dissociative identity disorder (AKA multiple personality disorder) have brain abnormalities, and the same is true even of people with Cotard's delusion, who think they are dead. But they are still singular, living people in spite of those abnormalities.

Finally, this indirectly proves that sex is biological. The claim that "the brain of a man who says he is a woman resembles a woman's brain" shows that there is a difference between people who say they are women ("transgender women") and people who simply are women ("biological women"). Both groups aren't simply called "women." The only way anyone could make this claim is if there is already a reference class called "biological women" that can be objectively determined and grouped together for brain scan experiments.

Preferred Pronouns?

Liberal Catholics also think that the failure to acknowledge someone by pronouns that reflect his gender identity (even if they contradict his biological sex) constitutes an attack on that person. Fr. Horan claims that "calling individuals by a name not of their choosing, let alone intentionally refusing to reference or address them by their preferred name or pronoun, is rude and hostile. I would add that such behavior is also unchristian and sinful."[70]

Why?

In one article in the *National Catholic Reporter*, Fr. Horan argues for "preferred pronouns" by piggybacking on the use of preferred names. He says that if Abram became Abraham, then we should have no problem with "embracing a new identity tied to a new nominal expression." But in Abram's case, *God* is the one who changed his name and assigned him a new mission.

Now, a person can change his name to signify a change he's made in life, such as a married woman taking her husband's surname or a bishop taking a papal name when he becomes pope. But pronouns represent facts about a person that no human being can change. I can no more become a "she," because of my immutable maleness, than I could become an "it" because of my immutable humanness.

Personally, I have no problem calling people by their name unless the name is something grossly offensive like "Lord Satan." (I also understand why someone would object to calling a man by a clearly feminine name who uses the name to reinforce a false identity.) What I do have a problem with, and Catholics should also be concerned about, is preferred *pronouns*.

You can't have your own pronouns any more than you can have your own adjectives. Those words refer to an objective reality about a person that can't be changed through our subjective preferences. Through hard work, we can change adjectives that describe some parts of our appearance, but whether a person is a "he" or a "she" is a biological reality. It is inscribed in every cell of our body—it is something, contrary to what our culture claims, that cannot be ignored in favor of our own preferences.

The Church does not have a teaching on whether it is sinful to use "preferred pronouns" when addressing someone. (I would say it is not prudent in the vast majority of cases.) But Fr. Horan goes beyond saying it is merely permissible to use this kind of language. He says it is obligatory under the pain of sin!

If this behavior were sinful, you'd think Fr. Horan could cite something from Scripture or the *Catechism* to defend his assertion. But the best he can come up with is saying the Golden Rule obliges us to use a person's preferred name and pronoun. For example, my full legal name is actually Trenton, but since middle school, I have preferred to go by *Trent*. So I agree with "Fr. Dan" (who has said he prefers that to "Daniel") that it would be rude if someone refused to call me by the name I prefer. ("Sinful," however, would be a stretch.)

But morality doesn't just boil down to a simple application of the Golden Rule.

I might want people to call me "Elvis Presley" because I have a mental illness and think I actually am "the King." It wouldn't be sinful for someone to refuse to call me by that name because he wants to restore my proper understanding of reality. Or, just because an anorexic might consider herself morbidly obese, that doesn't mean we should use her "preferred adjectives" like "overweight," because that's a lie in service of a delusion. The same is true for individuals who claim to be women but are actually men and *vice versa*: we shouldn't lie in service of a delusion that is harmful to their well-being.

Fr. Horan then halfheartedly recommends a kind of disobedience to priests and bishops who refuse to use preferred pronouns so that they "get a taste of their own medicine." He says,

> If they insist that disrespecting individuals and forcing them to respond to names or identities not of their choosing is the "Christian" path, then I suppose the same bishop wouldn't mind it if we called him "her" or "Sister Mary" instead of "Bishop So-and-so." Or, we should insist the school principal who prefers to be addressed as "Mrs. Smith" ought to be called "Bob" now.

When I speak about transgender issues, people online sometimes refer to me as "Mrs. Horn" in order to get a rise out of me. But, unlike some individuals who identify as transgender, I don't explode into a fit of rage when I'm "misgendered." My identity as a man isn't a fictitious construct whose existence depends on me convincing (or when that fails, threatening) others to accept it. My status as a man is a biological fact no one could change, so any attempt to do so elicits only mild amusement from me. Even *God* couldn't cause me to become a woman. He could make a woman who is a lot like me, but she would not be *me*. My maleness is like my species—it is an essential part of my identity, and I couldn't exist without it.

To put it simply, God couldn't turn "Trent Horn" into a woman any more than he could turn "Trent Horn" into a wombat.

Fr. Horan's examples fail because calling a male teacher "Mrs." or a bishop "Sister" is a *falsehood*. Even a bishop's title has more grounding in reality than a transgender individual's preferred pronouns, because a bishop's title refers to a part of reality that changed when he was ordained.

Horan also claims that critics who attack gender ideology "generally don't know what they are talking about. Such folks would do well to listen to leading scholars on the subjects of sex and gender, like Judith Butler of University of California, Berkeley, instead of attacking her and other experts."[71] I wonder if Fr. Horan would say Pope Benedict XVI "didn't know what he was talking about" when he criticized Butler for saying things like "the body is not 'sexed' in any significant sense prior to its determination within a discourse through which it becomes invested with an 'idea' of natural or essential sex."[72] In a 2008 address to the Roman Curia, he said, "What is often expressed and understood by the term 'gender' ultimately ends up being man's attempt at self-emancipation from creation and the Creator."[73]

An Outdated Binary?

In 2023, Fr. Horan's employer, the all-female St. Mary's College, announced it would accept "transgender female" students. The local bishop, Kevin Rhoades, urged the college to reverse a decision that he said "departs from fundamental Catholic teaching on the nature of woman and thus compromises its very identity as a Catholic woman's college." Thankfully, the college followed the bishop's counsel, which Fr. Horan protested, saying the failure to acknowledge the womanhood of "trans women" constitutes unjust discrimination.[74] Horan later quit the social media platform X (formally known as Twitter) because of the backlash he received for making what he called "a simple transgender-affirming post" in light of the controversy. He wrote, "trans women are women. . . . Just because it's new or confusing to you doesn't make it untrue or wrong or sinful or anything other than reality."[75]

This isn't "trans-affirming"—it's reality-denying.

Also, it's ironic that Fr. Horan complains about critics having no universal definition of "gender ideology" but sees no problem with transgender advocates having no universal definition of "woman." They don't even have *a definition* beyond useless circular ones like "a woman is anyone who claims to be a woman."

And Fr. Horan prefers this definitional anarchy: in his book *Catholicity and Emerging Personhood*, he says anthropologies that treat *man*, *woman*, and *human* as immutable, universal categories are based on outdated Thomistic philosophy. He cites the National Catholic Bioethics Center (NCBC), which he calls a "partisan think tank," as saying,

> A person's sex is manifested in the body in accordance with how the person has been created, and so it cannot be in conflict with any truer or deeper sexual identity contrary to the bodily sex. This is a foundational anthropological point that no medical association or political ideology can overturn.[76]

Fr. Horan says this approach "effectively reject[s] the reality of both gender dysphoria as a condition and transgender persons as such." But it does no such thing. The NCBC recognizes that there are people who experience dysphoria (or "bad feelings") with regard to the truth about whether they are a man or woman and may call themselves "transgender" as a result. It doesn't deny that transgender people exist, it just denies that transgender persons (and others who go along with them) are correct when they say things like "a woman can have a penis."

In contrast to the NCBC (and nearly everyone else in human history), Fr. Horan says we need to abandon an "essentialist" account of the human person and replace it with something that places the "individual" as the prime element of defining our personhood. Fr. Horan says this will bypass the "impasse" that arises from trying to categorize people in relation to "outdated" binary identities like *man* and *woman*.

But this account is doomed to fail, just like its secular counterparts. That's because, unlike ethnicity or race, sex truly is a binary concept. If race were binary, then it could be defined solely in terms, for argument's sake, of *whiteness* and *blackness*, but those terms can't define other distinct racial identities like being Asian. You can define being *Asian* without any reference to being white or black. But you can't define any of the dozens (if not hundreds) of alternative genders without reference to male or female. They all basically boil down to male, female, both, or neither. This reinforces that the issue of whether we are men or women is an objective sexual reality (not a subjective facet of "gender"), and that reality is binary, not just for human beings, but for any organism that engages in sexual reproduction.

This is a reality that is so ingrained into our being that every culture on earth has recognized it. Pope Francis has condemned modern cultures who seek to impose this error on other cultures through what he calls "ideological colonization." In a 2023 interview, he called it "one of the most dangerous ideological colonizations," and in a 2016 interview, he said,

Today children—children—are taught in school that everyone can choose his or her sex. Why are they teaching this? Because the books are provided by the people and institutions that give you money. These forms of ideological colonization are also supported by influential countries. And this is terrible![77]

Fr. Horan calls statements like these from Pope Francis "*ad hoc* statements signaling his personal displeasure." But what's truly *ad hoc* is Fr. Horan's habit of trumpeting the pope's teaching on issues like climate change but then explaining away his teaching on sex and gender. Hopefully, Fr. Horan will follow the pope's lead and show compassion to transgender individuals without jettisoning the revelation that each of us is beautifully made in God's image—male and female he created us.

6

THE PRO-LIFE MOVEMENT

In 2016, Rebecca Bratten Weiss, a former adjunct professor at the Franciscan University of Steubenville, co-founded an online movement called "the new pro-life movement." What was wrong with the old pro-life movement? In a 2019 interview she said, "We feel there is too much time spent arguing with the social and political figures who support abortion and not nearly enough time spent helping the women who actually have them."[78] Bratten Weiss also claimed that attempts to ban abortion don't have any effect on reducing abortion rates and should be scrapped in favor of programs that only help women with unintended pregnancies.

Similar Catholic pessimism toward banning abortion can be found in a 2020 article in *America* magazine, where William Cavanaugh claimed that pro-life politicians "failed to achieve the reversal of *Roe v. Wade* because they do not really want to" and that a new approach was needed.[79] He said that pro-life politicians would always keep abortion legal so that pro-lifers would keep voting for them in the vain hope of overturning *Roe v. Wade*. (Bratten Weiss admits she held this view as well.)

In my reply to Cavanaugh, published in *Catholic World Report*, I said, "Pro-lifers shouldn't give up on the Supreme Court" because the Court at least mitigated the evil of abortion and prevented its expansion. This can be seen in its upholding of partial-birth abortion bans and protecting the freedom of pro-lifers, such as in *NIFLA v. Becerra* (2018), where, in a 5-4 decision, California was prevented from forcing pregnancy centers to advertise abortion services.

When I wrote my reply to Cavanaugh in 2020, I didn't think *Roe v. Wade* would soon be overturned. After that happened, you'd think liberal Catholics would say they were wrong about it being "a waste of time" to try to overturn *Roe*. Instead, they showed their true colors: overturning *Roe* was not an impossible task to be abandoned; it was a morally wrong act to be rejected, because deep down, they always wanted abortion to remain legal.

Roe Isn't "Entirely" Evil?

Some liberal Catholics claim that the harms involved in outlawing abortion outweigh the harms involved in keeping it legal, and that's why something like *Roe v. Wade* can be called a "win" for Catholics. They cite Augustine's toleration of prostitution in order to keep lust from destroying the social order as one example where a Catholic can support the legality of a grave evil (*De Ordine* 2.4). However, the analogy fails because abortion involves an act of violence against an innocent person. Aquinas might have tolerated legal prostitution in order to prevent greater evils, but not grave acts of violence against the innocent like the rape and torture of children.

So what are these "greater harms" that require keeping abortion legal?

Bratten Weiss said abortion increases maternal mortality and worries that innocent women might be prosecuted for miscarriages.[80] On the latter point, some parents are falsely convicted of child abuse even though their born children died of natural causes (e.g., sudden infant death syndrome, or SIDS). Just as those miscarriages of justice don't justify repealing all laws against child abuse, improper application of abortion laws doesn't justify depriving all unborn children of legal protection. With regard to maternal mortality rates, countries with very restrictive abortion laws (like Poland) and even countries that simply have more restrictive laws (like Germany, Finland, and Denmark) have lower maternal mortality rates than the United States.[81]

Another proponent of the "Catholics should mourn *Roe v. Wade*" school of thought is Stephen Millies, a professor of public theology and director of the Bernardin Center. He claimed in his book *Good Intentions: A History of Catholic Voters' Road from Roe to Trump* that *Roe v. Wade* was "not entirely evil" because it "can be a sign of how the political system and the legal system are taking the rights of women in particular and persons more generally ever more seriously."[82]

When Millies publicly dialogued with me about this on my podcast, I asked him about *Dred Scott v. Sandford* (which upheld slavery) and *Plessy v. Ferguson* (which upheld racial segregation).[83] I said, "Are those [cases] evil, entirely evil, or do you think there were some good elements in those cases?" In response, Millies said, "Let me not walk into that trap." After I pressed him on the question, he eventually agreed that those cases were evil before quickly moving on with his argument. And yet Millies can't bring himself to say the same about cases like *Roe* or *Casey v. Planned Parenthood* that made it impossible to protect unborn children.

In an article he published after our dialogue, Millies said *Roe* can be considered good in some respects because it recognized competing interests between unborn children and pregnant women, a good he does not find in evil cases like *Plessy*. But *Plessy* acknowledges that there are competing interests between the need not to treat minorities as inferior and the need to respect private property rights and social customs.

Millies also claims that *Dobbs v. Jackson*, the case that led to the Supreme Court overturning *Roe*, is like *Plessy v. Ferguson* in that both allow individual states to regulate issues like abortion or segregation. He says this is unacceptable because "fundamental rights claims cannot depend on geography. Abortion either is a question about human life that can be compared to slavery and segregation, or it can be right for it to be adjudicated state by state. Both cannot be true."[84]

A situation where only some states allow abortion isn't ideal, but it is better than no state being free to protect the unborn. And we do have laws in the U.S. that allow for the protection of human life in some states but not others. *Dobbs* is more like *Glucksberg v. Washington* than *Plessy v. Ferguson*. *Glucksberg* (1999) was a 9-0 Supreme Court case that declared that there is no constitutional right to assisted suicide. *Glucksberg* did not strike down laws allowing assisted suicide, just as *Dobbs* did not force states to outlaw abortion. Instead, *Glucksberg* allowed each state to decide the legality of assisted suicide, and about a dozen so far have allowed the practice.

Is this ideal? No, but it is better than a decision that mirrors *Roe v. Wade* and makes assisted suicide a constitutional right imposed upon every state.

I also found it ironic in our dialogue that Millies said overturning *Roe* would be wrong because it would require the government to use power and coercion to get people to give up their bodily autonomy for the good of others.

After *Brown v. Board of Education* overturned *Plessy*, many people in the South were unwilling to accept its ruling. Consequently, President Dwight D. Eisenhower sent federal troops to escort black students to school. That sounds like government coercion to me!

When Millies and I discussed state coercion in the case of governments mandating masks and vaccines to combat COVID-19, we agreed that such coercion *could* be justified to preserve human life. But when I asked him if this same logic applied to abortion, he said, "They're not comparable in the way the pandemic is a pressing and present crisis, where thousands of people are dying every day," whereas abortion has been happening for fifty years. Against this distinction I reminded him that thousands of children have died every day from abortion for fifty years, and so abortion is truly a "pandemic" to the unborn.

Pro-abortion, "Catholic" Feminism

At a 2019 meeting of the Catholic Theological Society of America, University of San Diego professor Emily Reimer-Barry delivered an address entitled "Another Pro-Life Movement Is Possible."[85] But like Bratten Weiss's "new pro-life movement," this movement is pro-life in name only. It even goes further and indirectly praises abortion as a morally good kind of "self-care" for women.

Reimer-Barry begins her talk by criticizing a diocese in Pennsylvania for firing a female employee who became pregnant outside of wedlock and had no plans to marry the baby's father. Reimer-Barry calls the woman's situation a "double bind" because the diocese expected the woman not to have an abortion but also fired her for becoming pregnant. In other words, the woman is in a "lose-lose" situation: she either terminates the life of her child or gets terminated from her position.

Or we can say the woman is being held responsible for her actions in the same way we would hold a male employee responsible for his actions. If a Catholic school principal had an affair and impregnated his secretary, we wouldn't say he is in a "double bind" because his only options are getting fired or murdering his secretary to cover up his sin. We would say he should be held accountable for his actions. He certainly should not be rewarded because he heroically chose not to murder someone.

Contra Reimer-Barry, it is not the school who was failing to be pro-life for expecting its employees to follow basic moral standards like "don't fornicate." Instead, people who engage in fornication or adultery and bring children into existence outside of the safe and loving context of the marital act are the ones who are not pro-life. If being pro-life is about more than just opposing abortion (as liberal Catholics are fond of saying), then it is also about protecting unborn children from other acts of violence. This includes not just *ending* their lives unjustly, but also *starting* their lives unjustly through IVF, surrogates, prostitution, fornication, or adultery.

Reimer-Barry's address also exhibits all the hallmarks of ambiguous support for legal abortion. She says, "I do not challenge the magisterial teaching that there should always be a presumption against taking human life" rather than admitting that the Magisterium teaches that direct abortion is always wrong.[86] In a footnote, she qualifies this statement by saying, "Given space limitations I am unable in this context to identify the key distinctions between indirect and direct killing."

She then references Patricia Beattie Jung's article "Abortion and Organ Donation: Christian Reflections on Bodily

Life Support," which is basically a defense of Judith Jarvis Thomson's *violinist argument* for abortion. That article was published in an anthology co-edited by Fr. Charles Curran, whose dissent against the Church was so extreme that in 1988, the Vatican said he was "not suitable nor eligible to teach Catholic theology."[87]

Ironically, in trying to make a feminist argument for legal abortion, Reimer-Barry ends up making an *anti-feminist* argument that fails to treat women as responsible moral agents. For example, she calls "the choice to advocate against legal abortion" a "choice to restrict women's agency" and says women would be respected if they were treated as "subjects capable of being *persuaded* to the good" (emphasis in the original). She also claims that the Church gives men more "latitude" when it comes to making decisions about killing, so why doesn't it do the same with women? Here's how she puts it:

> Catholic theologian Christine Gudorf has noted that the Catholic tradition has given men wide latitude with respect to the ethics of war, but it has demonstrated mistrust of women when it comes to life-and-death decisions about pregnancy and childbirth. Gudorf explains that church leaders and theologians have recognized a legitimate diversity of moral opinions about state violence and warfare, all of which have been placed under the rubric of a respectable, morally principled debate. In the context of war, bishops acknowledge that decisions about killing are morally complex and should be approached through dialogue, moral education, and ongoing discernment. Gudorf asks, "Why is the same method not assumed to be appropriate in the context of women's decision-making around abortion?"

The problem with this argument is that the Church un-equivocally condemns the direct killing of innocent people in war (CCC 2313). Pope Francis has even suggested that most wars are unjust because of the harm they cause, even indirectly, to innocent human lives.[88] Moral theologians might debate whether there is a proportionate reason to risk innocent lives in a certain conflict, but they all agree that it would be a war crime if a soldier tried to depress enemy morale by executing all the children in a kindergarten class.

Men are also held accountable in a similar way when they kill *wanted* unborn children, such as when a husband kills his pregnant wife and is tried for two counts of murder. Yet, under Reimer-Barry's framework, women are apparently so unable to grasp the moral issues at hand that they have to be treated like small children who can't be held accountable in any meaningful way for the violence they willingly inflict upon other people through abortion.[89]

Abortion as "Self-care"?

The most outlandish part of Reimer-Barry's argument is her analysis of various "case studies" in obtaining abortions. One of them involves two people who get pregnant after a random hook up, get an abortion, and then stay in their relationship and have children later. The couple call their relationship a "nontraditional fairytale love story," while Reimer-Barry says, "We can respect Shelly and Paul's mu-tual discernment and celebrate the love they share today."[90]

This is morally perverse.

Even if there is some glimmer of morality in these ac-counts, since no human being is purely evil, there isn't any sense of sorrow for the deaths of these children or moral dis-approval of the selfishness that drove these parents to kill their children. Many people in worse circumstances manage not to harm their children, yet Reimer-Barry would probably consider it anathema ever to say a couple who choose abortion are being selfish. In fact, she approvingly cites someone who says, "The decision to abort is often a reflection of self-care. . . . Self-care is not the same thing as selfishness."

Even Michael Sean Winters of the *National Catholic Reporter* found Reimer-Barry's argument "fatally flawed." He writes, "Reimer-Berry begins by discussing violence, by which she means patriarchal violence, without actually acknowledging the violence of surgical abortion." He then says,

> The fact that this example made it into Reimer-Berry's talk and there was no general outcry is astonishing. How can we continue to defend the consistent ethic of life and then abandon our commitment to the life of the unborn? That would make us as hypocritical as the pro-lifers who support the death penalty. This is what I mean by the Catholic left suddenly losing its bearings.[91]

But it's not just Catholics who defend legal abortion that undermine the Church's teaching on the dignity of the unborn. Catholics who say dozens of other social issues are just as important as abortion can create a *de facto* defense of legal abortion by requiring pro-lifers to solve every problem facing born people before they are even allowed to legally protect unborn people—a point we will examine in detail in our next chapter.

7

THE PRE-EMINENCE OF ABORTION

In 2019, the U.S. Catholic bishops debated whether a letter accompanying their document on political life, "Forming Consciences for Faithful Citizens," should describe abortion as the "pre-eminent" moral issue facing Americans today. Some Catholics reject the language of "pre-eminence" because they fear that it will turn the faithful into mindless "single-issue" voters. Matthew Sitman writes at *Commonweal*, "By pointing to one issue as 'pre-eminent,' the bishops, as Francis might put it, are replacing consciences more than forming them. Catholics are not called to be single-issue voters but to serve the common good in all its complexity."[92]

But this reasoning doesn't survive scrutiny when we apply it to past injustices. If liberal Catholics admit that there were pre-eminent social issues in the past, then that same logic would apply to the bishop's description of abortion as the pre-eminent issue of our time.

Was Slavery "One Issue Among Many"?

It's the 1860 presidential election, and you have four candidates to choose from. Three of them want to allow the new states in the West to practice legal slavery. The fourth, Abraham Lincoln, says that the federal government should prevent these states from ever making it legal to enslave a human being. Whom do you vote for? I bet it's the candidate who opposes legal slavery.

Does that make you a naïve, "single-issue" voter?

After all, voters in 1860 were concerned about many important issues, including poverty, tariffs, women's rights, and secession. The few rogue abortionists who operated were also a concern. (The American Medical Association condemned them. How times have changed!)

Yet out of those issues, only one of them, *slavery,* was *pre-eminent.* It represented a colossal injustice to the four million people—13 percent of the population—who were legally enslaved. And none of the other injustices against blacks (like being deprived the right to vote) could be remedied without first addressing the evil of slavery. In fact, the same is true when it comes to offenses against human life today.

The Compendium of the Social Doctrine of the Church says, "Promoting human dignity implies *above all* [emphasis added] affirming the inviolability of the right to life, from conception to natural death, the first among all rights and the condition for all other rights of the person" (553). If the unborn can be victimized because they haven't become citizens through birth, then why can't migrants or other marginalized people be victimized for similar reasons? In a speech he gave to an Italian pro-life group in February of 2019, Pope Francis put it this way:

Those who have been conceived are children of the whole of society. Their killing in huge numbers, with the endorsement of states, is a serious problem that undermines the foundations of the construction of justice, compromising the proper solution of any other human and social issue.[93]

This doesn't mean we should ignore victimized born people, but we also shouldn't treat all social issues, or even all "life issues," as requiring equal political and pastoral responses. Even Cardinal Joseph Bernardin, whose "seamless garment" has been cited to make a "pro-life" issue out of every cause imaginable, said,

> I know that some people on the left, if I may use that label, have used the consistent ethic to give the impression that the abortion issue is not all that important anymore, that you should be against abortion in a general way but that there are more important issues, so don't hold anybody's feet to the fire just on abortion. That's a misuse of the consistent ethic, and I deplore it. But the misuse does not invalidate the argument.[94]

As the Church guides its members to promote justice in the world, we should prioritize those experiencing the worst injustices on the largest scale. Also, making abortion just "one issue among many" doesn't increase the urgency of addressing other issues—it just decreases the urgency of helping the unborn and justifies ignoring them.

Pre-eminence and Conscience

In a 2021 article for *America* magazine, Todd Salzman and Michael Lawler claim that describing abortion as the pre-eminent social issue of our time violates principles of conscience. They say, "Rather than focusing on the prohibition of individual acts like abortion, contraception, and same-sex marriage, the bishops should offer clear examples of moral principles like human dignity, the common good, and solidarity that would genuinely help Catholics to discern their votes conscientiously."[95]

Would it, though?

If you ask ten people to define "the common good" or "human dignity," you'll get at least eleven answers. It would be easy for uninformed Catholics to mistakenly think that so-called same-sex "marriage" promotes human dignity or that access to abortion is what's best for "the common good." It's also easy for Catholics who should know better to use these terms to obfuscate their dissent against Church teaching. For example, Salzman and Lawler say, "We do not know of a single Catholic voter who does not know what the church teaches on abortion and sexual ethical issues; we do know many Catholics who disagree with those teachings based on well-formed consciences."

Now, it's true that there are people who *claim* to have well-formed consciences who reject what the Church teaches on abortion or sexual ethics. But their consciences can't possibly be "well formed" if they reject a teaching that can't be wrong. For example, the *Catechism* says, "Since the first century the Church has affirmed the moral evil of every procured abortion. This teaching has not changed and remains unchangeable" (2271).

A conscience that leads someone to accept the moral permissibility of abortion is not well formed, just as a compass that always points south is not well calibrated. And, even though the Church has not infallibly defined the necessity of civil laws to prohibit abortion (something that wasn't a concern for nearly all of Church history), the Church does authoritatively teach that the State has a duty to pass such laws.

For example, when he served as an auxiliary bishop of San Diego, Cardinal Robert McElroy described "the [political] candidate who refuses to vote for any legal restrictions on abortion and argues that he is in fact doing more to reduce abortions by his support for aid to the poor and health care programs." McElroy concluded that "such a candidate has rejected the core substance contained in the Catholic teaching on abortion and civil law."[96] In another piece in *America* magazine, Charles Camosy and David McPherson call out Salzman and Lawler for missing this point:

> We are not told in what sense such consciences that deny prenatal human lives equal protection of the law are "well formed." This is an evaluative judgment that implies a position that does not in fact affirm a consistent life ethic. Again, would one say that a well-formed conscience could support white supremacy or policies that denied people of color equal protection of the law?[97]

The biggest problem for liberal Catholics who reject abortion as the pre-eminent issue of our time is that they refuse to provide any set of criteria to lay out which issues are not only *more* important, but the *most* important. If every issue is of equal importance, then you could justify any candidate for office who endorses grave evils by just pointing to any other issue, no matter how trivial, on which the candidate coheres with Catholic teaching: "Sure, Rep. Smith says illegal aliens should be shot on sight when they cross the border, but have you heard about his progressive tax proposal?"

However, if they do create a framework that acknowledges that some issues are more important than others, than any coherent framework will have abortion at the top of the list.

Reducing Abortion or Outlawing It?

Other Catholics claim that outlawing abortion should not be the Church's pre-eminent issue because outlawing abortion has little effect on reducing the number of abortions that occur. For example, Bratten Weiss asserts that "there is little evidence that banning abortion leads to reduced abortion rates."[98] However, a study published by the Institute of Labor Economics found that "in the first six months of 2023, births rose by an average of 2.3 percent in states enforcing total abortion bans compared to a control group of states where abortion rights remained protected, amounting to approximately 32,000 additional annual births resulting from abortion bans."[99]

Abortion rates dramatically decreased where abortion was banned and rose in neighboring states where it remained legal. And though some women still obtained abortions, not all did. The authors conclude that "one fourth of people seeking abortions did not receive them due to bans." This means that over 30,000 children who would have been killed were spared. And it's not as if abortion bans caused thousands of children to be aborted who would have lived if the bans had never been enacted. (Can you even think of a single child being aborted for that reason?)

Even before *Dobbs*, we knew that pro-life legislation saves lives. For example, after Texas banned abortions after six weeks of pregnancy in 2021, abortion rates decreased by 60 percent.[100] Sociologist Michael New has shown that even modest abortion restrictions, like waiting periods and informed consent laws, lead to a reduction in abortion rates.[101] According to *The Washington Post*, "states with more people who oppose abortion rights tend to have lower abortion rates."[102]

Low abortion rates in states like South Dakota are due in part to public demonstrations at abortion facilities, education campaigns, and pro-life legislation mandating informed consent laws and waiting periods. What should be common sense is borne out by statistics: in places with few abortion facilities and many pro-life advocates, bolstered by laws that make abortion more difficult to commit, there are fewer abortions. For example, Wyoming and Vermont have similar populations and household incomes, but whereas Vermont has six abortion facilities, Wyoming has only one. In 2017, 140 abortions were committed in Wyoming but 1,200—over eight times as many—in Vermont.[103]

To add an international perspective, many liberal Catholics say abortion rates would decrease if we adopted the economic policies of countries like Sweden that have generous entitlement programs. But Sweden has a higher abortion rate (about 19 per 1,000 women) than the United States (about 14 per 1,000 women), so this doesn't bode well for the claim that abortions would go away if poverty went away.[104]

A 2015 study found that women in extreme poverty are four times less likely to have an abortion than those in the lower middle class. The authors say, "Most unmarried women are sexually active, regardless of income. But women with higher incomes are much more successful at ensuring that sex does not lead to an accidental baby."[105] Poverty may certainly influence the decision to have an abortion, just as poverty may be more likely to influence other crimes like theft. But the data don't support the claim that abortion is merely a symptom of living in poverty. Abortion is also a *moral* and *legal* problem, since the poor rarely kill their newborns even when that might be more feasible than choosing abortion.

Dobbs was a necessary first step toward solving that problem, but it was never meant to be a panacea. Pro-life advocates have experienced setbacks at the ballot box and victories in state legislatures when it comes to protecting the unborn. It's also possible abortion rates could rise in the future due to other unforeseen factors, such as a greater push for chemical abortions delivered by mail in lieu of abortion facilities. But wherever the tides of politics and culture flow, it should always be our pre-eminent priority to ensure that every human being is treated with dignity and protected under the law.

8

CONTRACEPTION

Critics who reject the Catholic Church's teaching on contraception often cite the 1966 "Pontifical Commission on Birth Control" to justify their dissent. They say Pope Paul VI ignored the research of the commission he directed to determine if contraception is immoral. According to Celia Wexler, author of *Catholic Women Confront Their Church*,

> the commission, which included Catholic married couples and physicians, reportedly voted overwhelmingly to lift the Vatican's blanket ban on artificial birth control, and to permit married couples to prudently plan their families. But that hope was dashed in 1968, when Paul VI, writing in his encyclical, *Humanae Vitae* [On Human Life], once more declared artificial contraception "intrinsically wrong."[106]

Critics like Wexler say the faithful were harmed by the pope's fear of rejecting tradition when he should have listened to "the best theological minds" in the Church. Catholics for Choice puts it this way: "*Humanae Vitae* marked a turning point for the Catholic church, as Pope Paul rejected the theologically sound findings of his own Papal Birth Control

Commission in favor of a turn to rigid orthodoxy."[107]

Finally, Lawler and Salzman claim in a 2023 article that since nine bishops were on the commission to permit birth control, this shows that the Church's teaching on contraception can be changed. They say that the traditional teaching on contraception is something that "faithful, credible, mature and adult Catholic theologians have thoroughly deconstructed."[108]

The Truth About the Birth Control Commission

For many Catholics, Pope Pius XI's 1930 encyclical *Casti Connubii* laid the issue of contraception to rest. Pope Pius XII said his predecessor's condemnation of acts done to hinder the procreation of new life within the conjugal union "is in full force today, as it was in the past and so it will be in the future."[109] But by the 1960s, millions of American women, including many Catholics, were using the new FDA-approved birth control pill.

Some theologians claimed that, unlike condoms and diaphragms, the Pill did not create a physical barrier between the spouses during intercourse, so it could be a legitimate way to space children. They also said the Pill was needed to stop population increases that would, according to environmentalists like Paul Ehrlich, kill hundreds of millions through global famines (a threat that, by the way, never materialized for the Pill to neutralize).[110]

In response, Pope John XXIII created a committee to discuss the issue whose first meeting reaffirmed the conclusions of Popes Pius XI and XII on contraception but said the mechanics of the birth control pill required greater study before any conclusions about it could be reached. However, some bishops in Europe were teaching that couples could follow their conscience regarding use of the Pill precisely because the Church had not reached a definitive conclusion about it. In response, Paul VI reconvened the Pontifical Commission for the Study of Population, Family, and Births and added seven members, some of whom were notorious for their dissent against Church teaching.

When people speak about the commission, they often assume that the pope simply selected the best theologians in the Church, and so he should have followed whatever they recommended. But there is evidence that the pope wanted a commission that would give him arguments to test rather than advice to follow. The late moral theologian Germain Grisez, who worked behind the scenes to help future commission member Fr. John Ford defend Church teaching, told the Catholic News Agency,

[Paul VI] was perfectly happy to have a lot of people on the commission who thought that change was possible. He wanted to see what kind of case they could make for that view. He was not at all imagining that he could delegate to a committee the power to decide what the Church's teaching is going to be.[111]

Robert McClory confirms this in his book *Turning Point*, which chronicles the history of the commission from the perspective of an American married couple who were invited to join its later sessions. According to McClory (who supports changing Church teaching on contraception), the invitation to the progressive theologian Bernard Häring said, "It is the High Authority who has wanted diverse currents of opinion to be represented in the group. Yours are well known."[112]

One example of Häring's "diversity" was his claim that procreation could not be an essential end of sex because it is physiologically impossible for many acts of intercourse to

CONFUSION IN THE KINGDOM

result in pregnancy (such as when a woman has not ovulated). But this is like saying that learning is not an essential end of reading because it is impossible to remember everything we've read.

The committee eventually grew to over seventy members, though some members, like the future Pope John Paul II, Karol Wojtyla, could not attend due to Soviet travel restrictions. Two notable attendees were Patrick and Patty Crowley, the Catholic founders of the Christian Family Movement. The Crowleys said surveys they conducted among married couples showed that the rhythm method "did nothing to foster marital love" and provided no greater unity between the spouses. Colette Povin, another married woman invited to the commission, slammed temperature-based rhythm methods: "When you die, God is going to say, 'Did you love?' He isn't going to say, 'Did you take your temperature?'"[113]

A few members of the commission tried to steer the discussion away from the consequences of forbidding contraception and remind everyone of the far more serious consequences of allowing contraception. But when Jesuit priest Fr. Marcelino Zalba asked about "the millions we have sent to hell if these norms [in favor of contraception] were not valid," he was met with this flippant response from Patty Crowley: "Fr. Zalba, do you really believe that God has carried out all your orders?"[114]

The Majority and Minority Reports

By this point, the commission had moved far away from its original focus on the mechanics of the birth control pill. A majority of theologians, many of whom were moved by the stories of Catholics who felt that the prohibition on contraception harmed their marriages, claimed that contraception is not intrinsically evil, and they drafted an eleven-page report summarizing their position. Meanwhile, Fr. John Ford, along with a handful of other commission members, drafted their own 9,000-word defense of the Church's teaching. (This would later be called the "minority report," even though it was not an official document.)

The commission's main report (now called the "majority report") claimed that contraception is not intrinsically evil. It and the minority report were given to Paul VI on June 28, 1966. Four months later, the pope commented on the majority report, saying it carried "grave implications . . . which demanded logical considerations." Some members worried that the entire report would be buried, so they leaked it to the *National Catholic Reporter*.

Robert Kaiser, a journalist who reported extensively on the commission at the time, said that because of the leak, "people would have proof positive that authorities in the Church were not only divided but also leaning preponderantly to a new view of marriage and the family that did not condemn couples to hell for loving each other, no matter what the calendar said."[115]

Does the commission's report include irrefutable arguments, or a "new understanding" of marriage that overturns what the Church has always taught about the need not to eliminate the procreative end of the conjugal act? Not by a long shot.

The commission claimed that "developments" in the Church's teaching on sex (such as the primacy of expressing love) and social developments such as lower infant mortality rates make contraception acceptable even though it was condemned in the past. Testimonies such as those compiled by the Crowleys also made an indirect appearance in this statement from the majority report: "Then must be considered the sense of the faithful: according to it, condemnation of a couple to a long and often heroic abstinence as the means to regulate conception, cannot be founded on the truth."[116]

But the intrinsic morality of an act is not dependent on demographic facts or societal opinions. For example, the commission steadfastly rejected abortion as a way to space children, but modern dissidents say the Church should change this teaching, too, because women's place in society has changed and many Catholics who identify as pro-choice find it impossible to follow a complete ban on abortion.

Finally, the report gives what would become a standard interpretation among dissenters of Church teaching on the issue of contraception:

> It is not to contradict the genuine sense of this tradition and the purpose of the previous doctrinal condemnations if we speak of the regulation of conception by using means, human and decent, ordered to favoring fecundity in the totality of married life and toward the realization of the authentic values of a fruitful matrimonial community.

In other words, couples don't have to abstain from contraception because it is intrinsically evil. They just have to make sure their use of contraception does not affect "the fecundity in the totality of married life." Salzman and Lawler write,

> The majority report was based on the new interpersonal union model that emerged from the [Second Vatican] Council that focused on the total meaning of marriage and of sexual intercourse within the marriage relationship. The interpersonal model continues to be the judgment of the majority of Catholic theologians and the vast majority of Catholic couples.[117]

Unity Through Procreation

Catholic philosopher Paul Gondreau calls Salzman's and Lawler's descriptions of the traditional teaching on sexuality a caricature and criticizes their appeal to the bishops on the committee who voted in favor of contraception:

> Few know that the "consciences"—and subsequently the votes—of the nine bishops labored under an erroneous understanding of the science of contraception. They believed that the birth control pill acted not as a block or inhibition of the natural procreative process, but as a kind of medication that "helped nature" by prolonging the woman's natural period of infertility. (We know this from the testimony of Georges Cardinal Cottier, a close friend of the Swiss Dominican who served as the secretary of the papal commission.)[118]

Gondreau also takes Salzman and Lawler to task for reducing the traditional teaching on sexuality to just a concern about the marital act being procreative in nature. He says that although our existence as animals means that the sexual act is obviously ordered toward procreation (as it is in all other animals), human bodies exist not merely for animal purposes. He writes,

> [Because] we are not pure bodies, but incarnate (rational) spirits with an ordering to interpersonal love, human sexuality also owns an essential ordering to interpersonal unitive love. In brief, God has endowed us with a sexed design for the joint purpose of procreation and unitive love, as HV makes plain.

The traditional view of Catholic sexuality recognizes that sex is for the expression of marital love and it is unitive precisely because it involves the full gift of the spouses, including the gift of their respective fertility. That's why Pope Francis said in an address to a conference on natural family planning that "there is a need always to keep in mind the inseparable connection between the unitive and procreative meanings of the conjugal act. . . . When these two meanings are consciously affirmed, the generosity of love is born and strengthened in the hearts of the spouses, disposing them to welcome new life."[119]

This is true even if that fertility is temporarily absent due to a natural bodily process like hormonal cycles or permanently absent due to age or health conditions. In contrast, the interpersonal union model championed by Salzman, Lawler, and other dissenters isolates the marital act from marital love, and the two go together only in an accidental way.

Concerning the majority report, what does it mean to use contraception "too much," to the point that it affects "the fecundity in the totality of married life"? Do couples have to make sure only that they use contraception for nearly all but not every sexual act? Do they just have to allow 51 percent of conjugal acts to have the possibility of conception? Or would simply having the standard 2.1 children suffice?

Imagine if someone claimed that occasional instances of adultery weren't wrong as long as they were being used as a means to strengthen the *overall* unity of the marriage (e.g., a husband wanting to boost his confidence so he can better love his wife). Should we demand that every single sexual act be faithful or promote "the faithfulness in the totality of married life"?

If that reasoning doesn't justify occasional acts of adultery, then it doesn't justify occasional acts of contraception. Philosopher Ralph McInerny also offers this helpful response: "The principle of totality cannot ground the claim that singular acts which, taken as such are offensive, cease to be so when considered in the light of the moral life taken as a whole. The moral imperative is not that we should act well more often than not. Rather it is: do good and avoid evil."[120]

In the section of *Humanae Vitae* on "Unlawful Birth Control Methods," Pope Paul VI addresses those who would defend the use of contraception for the end of promoting the overall good of the marriage:

> Though it is true that sometimes it is lawful to tolerate a lesser moral evil in order to avoid a greater evil or in order to promote a greater good, it is never lawful, even for the gravest reasons, to do evil that good may come of it—in other words, to intend directly something which of its very nature contradicts the moral order and which must therefore be judged unworthy of man, even though the intention is to protect or promote the welfare of an individual, of a family, or of society in general. Consequently, it is a serious error to think that a whole married life of otherwise normal relations can justify sexual intercourse which is deliberately contraceptive and so intrinsically wrong (14).

The members of the Pontifical Birth Control Commission who dissented against Church teaching may have envisioned a Church that compromised only on contraception but upheld other longstanding traditions on Catholic sexual morality, such as opposition to homosexual conduct. But notice the ominous way Salzman and Lawler conclude their piece: "Once the Church recognizes the flaws in *Humanae Vitae*'s foundational principle, the entire edifice of official Catholic sexual teaching crumbles."

Given how society's reverence for sexuality has crumbled since *Humanae Vitae* (a fact Paul VI predicted in that encyclical), Catholics must defend all the Church's teachings on sexuality, lest the faithful's reverence for God's gift of our sexuality crumble in the same way. This includes defending it from outright dissenters like Salzman and Lawler and even challenging bishops who undermine this teaching.

In 2022, the Pontifical Academy for Life published *Theological Ethics of Life: Scripture, Tradition, Practical Challenges*, which contained a paper from some theologians arguing that it is moral in some cases for married couples to contracept the sexual act. Archbishop Vincenzo Paglia, the head of the Academy, called the work a "paradigm shift" in moral theology in the introduction he penned for it.[121] But a year later, when asked about *Humanae Vitae*'s teaching that "any action specifically intended to prevent procreation is not permissible," Paglia seemed to backtrack: "I am in agreement with every provision of *Humanae Vitae*. You will find no one who defends life more fiercely and tenaciously than I do."[122]

We shouldn't be surprised that confusion among theologians, and even among some bishops, on the issue of contraception has persisted over fifty years since the teaching was clearly reaffirmed in *Humanae Vitae*. In spite of the clear teachings of the Council of Nicaea in 325, Arian and other Christological heresies plagued the Church for centuries (and still exist in some forms). In all these cases, the faithful must avoid two extremes: sinful despair, which nullifies Christ's promise to protect the Church from the gates of hell, and foolish optimism, which thinks the Holy Spirit acts alone, without any cooperation from the faithful's courageous witness, to protect the Church from teaching error.

Instead, we should recall St. Paul's words to the church of Corinth, which was also plagued with troubles: "Be steadfast, immovable, always abounding in the work of the Lord, knowing that in the Lord your labor is not in vain" (1 Cor. 15:58).

9

GOD THE MOTHER?

As someone who has defended the unborn against pro-abortion attacks for over twenty years, when I hear the word *feminism* or *feminist*, the hair on the back of my neck stands up. My guard is raised because modern feminism is almost always associated not with the laudable goal of affirming the dignity of women, but with promoting evils like abortion, contraception, and marginalization of fathers.

But that doesn't mean I think all feminism is evil.

I've partnered with groups like Feminists for Life, who oppose abortion in the same spirit as "first wave feminists" like Susan B. Anthony and Elizabeth Cady Stanton, who saw abortion as exploitative of women. Although not everything they supported was good, society improved after first wave feminists helped women attain full legal personhood by securing rights such as the right to vote. I also agree with Pope St. John Paul II that

> in transforming culture so that it supports life, women occupy a place, in thought and action, which is unique and decisive. It depends on them to promote a "new feminism" which rejects the temptation of imitating models

of "male domination," in order to acknowledge and affirm the true genius of women in every aspect of the life of society, and overcome all discrimination, violence, and exploitation (*Evangelium Vitae* 99).

This genius can be seen in thoughtful female exegesis of biblical texts that men often overlook. For example, most people describe Bathsheba's encounter with King David as an "affair" or act of adultery. But if we condemn Hollywood creeps like Harvey Weinstein for using their power and authority to coerce women into sexual acts, then we should be willing to view King David in a similar light, who had even more power over a common Israelite woman. When it is seen in this framework, Bathsheba becomes a victim of David's predation and not a "temptress" or accomplice to adultery.

But although insights like these can be helpful, "feminist theology" more often introduces ideas that don't build up the kingdom of God, but tear it down because it is a "patriarchal" kingdom.

Many of the evils we've discussed so far, such as sodomy and abortion, are rooted in feminist theology that denies essential differences between men and women and promotes abortion as a moral good for women. But before it reaches such an alarming juncture, feminist theology begins more fundamentally, with proposals to change the traditional language the Church has used to describe God the Father.

Our Mother in Heaven?

According to the group's website, "Catholic Women Preach" offers reflections on texts from the liturgical year with a "special emphasis on the lives of women, their apostolic call, and their roles in the Church and the world." Most people haven't heard of these reflections because these feminist preachers have succeeded in their quest for equality and now pen homilies as forgettable as the ones male priests give on the same readings. However, a few of these reflections managed to push the envelope and get shared on things like Fr. Martin's Twitter page. One of them, from a high school campus minister named Vicky McBride, said,

> Did I believe that god would reveal herself to me in this new state I found myself in? In the readings this week god reveals herself to several people in dramatic and surprising ways. . . . It is good that we are here in whatever state we find ourselves in because god is with us and prepared to reveal herself to us. . . . Sit and be with god and god will let you glimpse her power.[123]

In a follow-up article at *America* magazine, Fr. Martin said, "I considered commenting, 'I was simply reposting the summary from Catholic Women Preach.' But that would imply I had a problem calling God 'Her.' And I don't."[124] Martin then cited feminist theologian Elizabeth Johnson, who claims that the masculine, Hellenistic concept of God as *logos* or "word" eventually "won out" over the Jewish concept of God as "wisdom" or *sophia*, which often invokes female imagery and uses a female noun.

First, the grammatical gender of a word tells us nothing about whether the concept behind the word is male or female. In biblical Hebrew, the word for army, *sava*, is a feminine noun even though ancient armies were composed almost entirely of men. In Hebrew, God's spirit (*ruach*) is a feminine noun, but Jesus refers to the Holy Spirit using the neuter noun *pneuma*, which lacks gender, and he explicitly calls the Holy Spirit "the helper" (*parakleton*), which is a male noun.

Second, the idea that God is to be identified with "Word" or "logos" is not something a Greek theological "boys' club" imposed upon the Church. God himself revealed that "in the beginning was the Word, and the Word was with God, and the Word was God" (John 1:1). Attributing this truth to misogyny leads to a denial of divine revelation and, consequently, of God himself.

Indeed, Johnson's descriptions of God are so problematic that in 2011, she earned a formal rebuke from the USCCB. The bishops said the theology in her book *Quest for the Living God: Mapping Frontiers in the Theology of God* "does not accord with authentic Catholic teaching on essential points." Concerning the use of male and female names for God, the bishops note the following:

> When the book speaks of the traditional masculine language for God, however, it is to denounce it as a tool of patriarchal oppression "religiously inadequate" for our times. . . . Is it unreasonable for the reader to find in these pages a call to replace inadequate, though traditional, language for God with feminine language?[125]

Metaphor and Analogy

Fr. Martin defends Johnson's language by pointing out that the Bible contains female symbols and language to describe God, such as comparing God to a nursing mother (Num. 11:12). However, Martin fails to mention that whereas the Bible often says God is *like* a mother in emotions like tenderness, it simply calls God "Father." Jesus teaches us to address God as "our Father" rather than mother, which was countercultural in an ancient world steeped in goddess worship, as can be seen in Acts 19's description of St.

Paul causing a riot because he disrupts worship of Artemis among the Ephesians. The *Catechism* says we must not confuse the inexpressible image of God with human representations (42). Moreover,

> in no way is God in man's image. He is neither man nor woman. God is pure spirit in which there is no place for the difference between the sexes. But the respective "perfections" of man and woman reflect something of the infinite perfection of God: those of a mother and those of a father and husband (370).

That means we must strictly distinguish *metaphorical* language about God, such as God being a nursing mother, from *analogical* language about God that explains God's unique nature through familiar aspects of his creation.

A metaphor simply says one thing is another thing, whereas an analogy explains the *relationship* between two different things. When I say, "This computer is a dinosaur," I metaphorically mean that the computer is really old. I could have picked any number of old things as a comparative noun, and my point would be the same. Aside from old age, computers have nothing in common with dinosaurs.

But when I say, "The computer can't read my handwriting on this check," I'm speaking analogically. A computer doesn't sound out words or recall phonics lessons as you and I do when we read. But a computer does identify text and written patterns in a way that is similar to what humans do. My description of a computer "reading text" would therefore be analogical language and not metaphorical.

When we say "God is good," we aren't speaking metaphorically. We also aren't speaking univocally, or saying "God is good" in the same way a steak might be good or even a person might be good. Created things are "good" if they conform to their essence—like when the steak is cooked enough but not too much, or when a person practices virtue. But God doesn't have to live up to a standard in the same way a person or a steak does. God just *is* the standard of goodness by which everything else exists. God's goodness is not *identical* to creaturely goodness, but it is *analogous* to it. It is similar enough for us to understand that God is perfect goodness itself.

So, when it comes to the use of female or male imagery to describe God, feminist theologians err when they treat masculine imagery describing God as mere metaphors. The masculine imagery is analogical in nature because it reveals truths about God by comparing him to human fathers. One of those truths is that God is the transcendent Creator, who made everything from nothing. Whereas a mother contains life inside her own body, a father creates life outside of himself. The *Catechism* makes a similar point, which Fr. Martin never engages in his article defending Johnson. It says,

> By calling God "Father," the language of faith indicates two main things: that God is the first origin of everything and transcendent authority; and that he is at the same time goodness and loving care for all his children.

The *Catechism* goes on to say that God is neither man nor woman, but God's tenderness can be expressed through images of motherhood. However, it ends by declaring that "no one is father as God is Father" (239).

Finally, Cardinal Ratzinger makes it clear that this analogical language is not something human beings invented for their own purposes. Instead, this language is part of divine revelation, which human beings have no authority to change:

But Christianity is not a philosophical speculation; it is not a construction of our mind. Christianity is not "our" work; it is a Revelation . . . and we have no right to reconstruct it. Consequently, we are not authorized to change the Our Father into an Our Mother; the symbolism employed by Jesus is irreversible; it is based on the same Man-God relationship that he came to reveal to us.[126]

The Necrophilia of Patriarchy?

Though feminist theologians are quick to dismiss masculine divine imagery as mere metaphors, their female descriptions of God get stretched to the breaking point. God becomes a *de facto* goddess or, more accurately, a divine self-projection. Sr. Joyce Rupp, a popular Catholic retreat leader, says this about "Sophia" the divine wisdom:

I count on Sophia to influence my attitudes, values, and beliefs, to help me make good choices and decisions. I pray to her each day to guide me as I try to reflect her love in all I am and all I do. Whenever I am in doubt as to how to proceed in my work and relationships, I turn to Sophia for wisdom and courage. She has never failed to be there for me.[127]

Throughout Church history, there have always been those who were not satisfied with God's self-revelation and decided to create a god (or goddess) in their own image to replace him. The fourth-century *Acts of Thomas* (which has no historical connection to the apostle Thomas) describes the apostle uttering this eucharistic prayer: "Come the hidden mother. Come, she that is manifest in her deeds and giveth joy and rest unto them that are joined under her.

Come and communicate with us in this Eucharist, which we celebrate in thy name."[128]

Other feminist theologians believe that "feminizing God" is putting lipstick on a pig. At the end of the day, you still have a patriarchal and oppressive divine being, even if it is wrapped up in gender-inclusive language. This can be seen in the works of Mary Daly, a former theology professor at Boston College who left the school in 1999 because she refused to allow men into her graduate seminars. In her book *Gyn/Ecology: The Metaethics of Radical Feminism*, she says,

> There is no way to remove male masculine imagery from God. Thus, when writing, speaking anthropomorphically of ultimate reality of the divine spark of being, I now choose to write gynomorphically. I do so because God represents the necrophilia of patriarchy. Whereas goddess affirms the life loving being of women in nature.[129]

If women represent "life loving being" to Daly, then men represent a kind of "life draining being," even when they are still in the womb. Daly is an avid supporter of legal abortion because that is the only way women can liberate themselves from "the Patriarchy," whose male members

> deeply identify with "unwanted fetal tissue," for they sense as their own condition the role of controller, possessor, inhabitor [sic] of women. Draining female energy, they feel "fetal." Since this perpetual fetal state is fatal to the Self of the eternal mother (Hostess), males fear women's recognition of this real condition, which would render them infinitely "unwanted."[130]

Good grief. Could Daly even entertain the possibility that men oppose abortion for the same reason many *women* oppose abortion: that it is wrong to kill innocent human beings? Perhaps their natural, masculine desire to protect the vulnerable is what motivates them to oppose the legal dismemberment of small children if not the human desire to be a civilized person.

No, Daly would say, because she claims any negative feelings women might have regarding abortion (including about their own abortions) comes from Christianity's false understanding of God as "the God who is the judge of sin." She writes, "Women have suffered both mentally and physically from this deity in whose name they have been informed that birth control and abortion are unequivocally wrong . . . that they must be present as rituals and services in which men have all the leadership roles."[131]

In other words, feminist theologians reject a "God" whose toxic masculinity reigns over the universe and wisely orders it. They prefer a "goddess" who fits neatly into one of their women's and gender studies seminars. Daly even subjugates Jesus to the goddess, saying, "Christ assimilates/devours the Goddess. . . . The gentle Jesus who offers the faithful his body to eat and his blood to drink is playing Mother Goddess."[132]

And when it comes to the argument that God became a man and chose men to be priests, Daly undercuts the entire thing by asserting that "the problem lies in the exclusive identification of this person with God in such a manner that Christian conceptions of divinity and of the 'image of God' are all objectified in Jesus."[133]

Daly advocated for female priests, but she also said in a 1968 interview, "I don't think it will be any panacea to go out and ordain women."[134] Swapping out women for men doesn't change the patriarchal underpinnings of the God priests represent as an *alter Christus*. For some feminist theologians, even the concept of priests as mediators between God and man is oppressive. This can be seen in a 2021 *Commonweal* article by Mary Kate Holman entitled "Priesthood reimagined." Holman notes that

> while women-priests proclaim their resistance to clericalism at every turn, it nonetheless remains a serious challenge for their ministry. . . . If women-priests claim an indelible essential transformation, they fall into the clerical power trap they seek to avoid. If they do not claim a transformation, they may lose some of their ordained authenticity.[135]

If patriarchy literally subjugates women, then these liberal dissenters who want to be female priests are really not at all different from nineteenth-century women who wanted to have equality with men by owning slaves. The only way out of this dilemma is to abandon the presumption that the Church is egalitarian and democratic. The Church instead contains a sacred order, or a "hierarchy," instituted by God to lead God's people to salvation.

Now you see how conclusions of a radical theologian like Daly often begin with the seemingly innocuous questions asked by a more muted liberal Catholic. The writings of feminist theologians like Daly show us that, to bring clarity amid the confusion of liberal Catholicism, we can't engage only the confusion they create around moral issues like sex and abortion. We must also clarify the confusion they sow regarding the foundations of our faith like Christ, the Eucharist, and Scripture—a task we now turn to in part two of this book.

PART II

FAITH AND JUSTICE

10

A UNIVERSAL CHRIST?

If you've attended a Catholic retreat, especially at a retreat center run by the Franciscan order, then you've probably seen a book or two in the center's bookstore by Franciscan Friar Fr. Richard Rohr. The most prominent one you'll see is probably his 2019 *New York Times* best-seller *The Universal Christ: How a Forgotten Reality Can Change Everything We See, Hope For, and Believe.*

Given that it's endorsed by Melinda Gates, Oprah, and Bono, surely it must be a sound presentation of Catholic orthodoxy! Granted, Bono's endorsement actually provides the most succinct summary of the book's central themes: "Rohr sees the Christ everywhere, and not just in people. He reminds us that the first incarnation of God is in Creation, and he tells us that 'God loves things by becoming them.'"

The Universal Christ was published in the spring of 2019 at the same time as my book *Counterfeit Christs: Finding the Real Jesus Among the Impostors* was published. If Rohr's book had been published just a few months earlier, I would have included Rohr's "universal Christ" among the counterfeits because it is just a repackaging of a heresy that has been with the Church since the Apostolic Age.

Is My Bookcase Christ?

One of the central themes of Rohr's book is that people have lost sight of "Christ" and must distinguish "Christ" from "Jesus" in order to fully connect with a personal and transcendent God. Rohr puts it this way: a merely personal God becomes tribal and sentimental, and a merely universal God never leaves the realm of abstract theory and philosophical principles. But when we learn to put them together, Jesus and Christ give us a God who is both personal and universal.[136]

If you know basic theology, this should sound strange to you because "Jesus" is the name given to the divine person who was born of Mary, and "Christ" is a title given to that same person that means "anointed one." It's like saying "Francis and the pope teach us about God"—it's either a bizarre redundancy or a division that makes two persons out of one person. And indeed, that seems to be the heresy that Rohr clumsily peddles throughout *The Universal Christ*. This can be seen in passages where Rohr speaks as if "Jesus" and "Christ" are two separate people, such as when he says, "Jesus and Christ are both the CliffsNotes read on Reality"[137] and "Jesus and Christ give us a God who is both personal and universal."

Astoundingly, even though the word "Christ" is mentioned over 400 times in *The Universal Christ*, Rohr spends only a few paragraphs explaining what the word "Christ" means. The *Catechism* says, "The title 'Christ' means 'Anointed One' (Messiah). Jesus is the Christ, for 'God anointed Jesus of Nazareth with the Holy Spirit and with power' (Acts 10:38). He was the one 'who is to come' (Luke 7:19), the object of 'the hope of Israel' (Acts 28:20)" (CCC 453).

In *The Universal Christ*, the term "anointed one" is mentioned three times. "Messiah" is mentioned only once, and in those descriptions, the "anointed one" is *not* Jesus. Instead, the anointed ones are everything else in Creation:

> The Christ Mystery anoints all physical matter with eternal purpose from the very beginning. (We should not be surprised that the word we translate from the Greek as Christ comes from the Hebrew word *mesach*, meaning "the anointed" one, or Messiah. He reveals that all is anointed!) . . . We all know reverence because it softens our gaze. Any object that calls forth respect or reverence is the "Christ" or the anointed one for us at that moment.

All created things are good because God made them (Gen. 1:18), but not everything is God's "anointed." My bookcase does a good job holding up my stuff, but it isn't "Christ." That title belongs to those who received God's anointing in the Old Testament, like Israel's kings (Ps. 28:8, 1 Sam. 24:1–6), and to those who have been anointed with the sacrament of confirmation Christ gave us (CCC 1289), and to Christ, who is the perfect "anointed one."

When Rohr tries to make everything "God's anointed," he slides into the error of pantheism. But before we discuss that heresy about Creation, we need to analyze an ancient error about Jesus that Rohr's language exacerbates.

In the second century, Gnostic heretics divided the Redeemer into two people: a human Jesus and the divine Christ he received later in his ministry. St. Irenaeus exposed these errors (and many others) in a five-volume work, appropriately titled *Against Heresies*. What he says of the Gnostics could just as easily apply to Rohr:

The gospel, therefore, knew no other Son of Man but him who was of Mary, who also suffered; and no Christ who flew away from Jesus before the Passion; but him who was born it knew as Jesus Christ the Son of God, and that this same suffered and rose again, as John, the disciple of the Lord, verifies, saying, "But these are written, that you might believe that Jesus is the Christ, the Son of God, and that believing you might have eternal life in his name"—foreseeing these blasphemous systems that divide the Lord, as far as lies in their power, saying that he was formed of two different substances (3.16.5).

In the early Church, Christians referred to the Blessed Virgin Mary as *Theotokos* or "God-bearer" to emphasize that the human Jesus and the divine Son were the same person. St. Gregory of Nazianzus said, "Whoever does not accept Holy Mary as the Mother of God has no relation with the Godhead."[138] However, the Nestorian heretics took up Gregory's challenge and rejected *Theotokos* in favor of *Christokos*, claiming that Mary gave birth to a human messiah who was joined in a "moral union" with the divine Son of God. (This view was formally condemned at the Council of Ephesus in 431.)

Jesus vs. Christ?

Is Rohr a Nestorian? Like many of the things he writes in his book, the answer isn't clear. Rohr refers to Mary being given the title *Mother of God* and says, "She is invariably offering us Jesus, God incarnated into vulnerability and nakedness."[139] But in other parts of his book Rohr seems to contradict himself when he distinguishes Jesus from the "divine Christ" as if they were two different persons:

The full Christian leap of faith is trusting that Jesus together with Christ gave us one human but fully accurate window into the Eternal Now that we call God. This is a leap of faith that many believe they have made when they say "Jesus is God!" But strictly speaking, those words are not theologically correct. Christ is God, and Jesus is the Christ's historical manifestation in time.

Except that St. Paul tells us that at the name of "Jesus," every knee will bow (Phil. 2:10) and that Jesus is Lord (Rom. 10:9). The *Catechism*, contra what Rohr might say, says that "the title 'Lord' indicates divine sovereignty. To confess or invoke Jesus as Lord is to believe in his divinity" (455). But Rohr gives divine praise to "Christ" while downplaying the human Jesus. He even undermines the appropriateness of worshiping Jesus as God:

> You have to trust the messenger before you can trust the message, and that seems to be the Jesus Christ strategy. Too often, we have substituted the messenger for the message. As a result, we spent a great deal of time worshiping the messenger and trying to get other people to do the same. . . . He did ask us several times to follow him, and never once to worship him.[140]

This is what Muslims say about Jesus. They claim that Jesus was a prophet who was "just a messenger" who wanted us to worship God. But in the Gospels, Jesus receives divine worship and doesn't reject it, which is remarkable since the New Testament describes other creatures being worshiped as God who either rightly reject the worship (like Paul and Barnabas in Acts 14) or wrongly accept it (like Herod in Acts 12). But when Thomas calls Jesus "my Lord and my

God," Jesus does not rebuke him, nor is Jesus rebuked, because Jesus, and not just "Christ," is our Lord and God.

Rohr also claims that "Christ" pre-existed Jesus and so "Christ cannot be coterminous with Jesus."[141] It is true that, prior to the Incarnation, God the Son did not have a human nature. But the *person* we call "Jesus" who had a human nature and the *person* of the Son who is eternally begotten by the Father are the same *person*. That's why Jesus could say in John 17:5, "Father, glorify thou me in thy own presence with the glory which I had with thee before the world was made." And because they are the same person, Rohr is simply wrong when he says, "My personal belief is that Jesus' own human mind knew his full divine identity only after his resurrection."[142]

Jesus did grow in knowledge that could be acquired only by human experience (such as carpentry skills), but he did not grow in his understanding of himself. The *Catechism* makes this clear in paragraph 474 where it says, "Christ enjoyed in his human knowledge the fullness of understanding of the eternal plans he had come to reveal," and this by his human knowledge's "union to the divine wisdom in the person of the Word incarnate."

I'm God Having a Human Experience?

Rohr also divides the person of Jesus in his chapter on the Eucharist, where he comments on Jesus' saying of the Passover bread, "This is my body" and telling the crowds, "My flesh is true food." Rohr writes, "He is giving us his full Jesus-Christ self—that wonderful symbiosis of divinity and humanity."

Rohr's use of the term "symbiosis" makes it seem as though Christ's human and divine natures are like two different entities that mutually benefit each other, like the "symbiosis" between a clownfish and a sea anemone. Once again, we are creeping into the Nestorian heresy that divides Christ into two persons: the human Jesus and the divine Christ. That's why, in the midst of the Nestorian heresy, the ecumenical Council of Chalcedon said,

> We confess that one and the same Christ, Lord, and only-begotten Son, is to be acknowledged in two natures without confusion, change, division, or separation. The distinction between the natures was never abolished by their union, but rather the character proper to each of the two natures was preserved as they came together in one person. It's also why the *Catechism*, quoting the Council of Trent, says, "In the most blessed sacrament of the Eucharist 'the body and blood, together with the soul and divinity, of our Lord Jesus Christ and, therefore, the whole Christ is truly, really, and substantially contained.'"

Rohr's treatment of the Eucharist reveals again his tendency toward pantheism, the view that God and the universe are the same thing, or *panentheism*, the view that God is the "soul" of the universe. For example, he claims of the Eucharist that "a true believer is eating what he or she is afraid to see and afraid to accept: the universe is the Body of God, both in its essence and in its suffering." He also utters this piece of Zen nonsense: "We are not just humans having a God experience. The Eucharist tells us that, in some mysterious way, we are God having a human experience!"[143]

Rohr's defenders often say he comes from a mystical tradition, so his words shouldn't be taken literally if they sound heretical. Rohr even instructs his readers to "allow some of the words in this book to remain partially mysterious, at least for a while."[144] But although mystery is an indispensable part of contemplating the God who is infinite being itself, it is a hindrance rather than a necessity in explaining the basics of our theology to another person. There's no excuse for this because the Eastern Fathers, like St. Athanasius, also wrote about the incomprehensible mysteries of God while clearly affirming Christian orthodoxy.

For example, Athanasius says the Son of God "leaves nothing devoid of his power but gives life and keeps it in being throughout all of creation and in each individual creature." But in affirming that God sustains the universe in existence, Athanasius is clear that God is not *identical* to the universe. One way he does this is by defending the teaching that God created the universe from nothing. He tells his pagan critics that "if [God] only worked up existing matter and did not himself bring matter into being, he would be not the Creator but only a craftsman."[145]

Rohr affirms that God created from nothing, but then he talks about how God "loves things by becoming them," "God's loving union with physical creation," and how "God joined in unity with the physical universe and became the light inside of everything."[146]

As heretical as this sounds, you could (if you strain your eyes really hard) write it off as an overly literal description of God's omnipresence—God sustaining and being causally present in all things rather than being the cold and distant God of deism. Maybe you could . . . until you hear Rohr talk about the "first" and "second" Incarnations.

The Second Incarnation?

One concept that is unique to Rohr's work is his belief that Creation represents "the first Incarnation." He writes, "This self-disclosure of whomever you call God into physical creation was the first Incarnation (the general term for any enfleshment [sic] of spirit). . . . Creation is the First Bible."[147]

Once again, we have to sift the half-truths from the false-hoods.

Our grand, orderly universe does reveal that an all-powerful God created it. It's why St. Paul says, "Ever since the creation of the world his invisible nature, namely, his eternal power and deity, has been clearly perceived in the things that have been made" (Rom. 1:20). But just as a painter's existence is revealed without him *becoming* the work of art he made, God is revealed through Creation without becoming a part of it.

If Rohr is using the literal sense of "incarnation," God becoming matter, then he's endorsing pantheism. The Pontifical Council for Interreligious Dialogue says, "There is no space in this view for God as a distinct being in the sense of classical theism."[148] Moreover, God has a rational nature, so he can't become "incarnate" in a non-rational substance like a tree, even though he can be causally present in a tree and sustain its existence.

Or, if Rohr is using the term in a metaphorical way, then this only serves to diminish the real Incarnation in Bethlehem. When Rohr asks, "What if Christ is another name for everything—in its fullness?", he isn't inspiring people to treat the universe the way they treat Christ; he's inspiring them to treat Christ like the universe, or to view Jesus Christ as a beautiful reality that is not God, but leads us to God. Describing Creation as the "first Incarnation" also contradicts the *Catechism*'s recognition of the "*unique and altogether singular event* [emphasis added] of the Incarnation of the Son of God" (464).

Rohr defends his view by citing Colossians 3:11: "Christ is all, and in all." But in that passage, St. Paul is saying that everyone is capable of receiving Christ in spite of social division. Paul admonishes the Colossians to stop slandering one another and to put off "the old nature" because "there cannot be Greek and Jew, circumcised and uncircumcised, barbarian, Scyth'ian, slave, free man, but Christ is all, and in all" (vv. 9–11)

In other words, Christ is in *all kinds* of people, so the body of Christ should not be divided by human social categories. Christ came to save all people. But Rohr's Christ is not a perfectly just God who mercifully saves us from sin. He is, rather, a non-threatening life force who, if we just saw him in the sunset, would inspire us to stop evildoers like corporations. Seriously, that's what he says:

> Evil is not just individual nastiness. "Our battle is not against human forces, but the Sovereignties and Powers that originate in the darkness, the spirits of evil in the air" (Eph. 6:12). We now see that these systems (corporations, nation-states, institutions) have a life of their own.[149]

To Hell with This . . .

It's not surprising that Rohr fails to accept St. Paul's references to demons ("spirits of evil in the air") because he doesn't believe that demons exist, apart from our own disordered feelings:

> Most people I know are overly identified with their own thoughts and feelings. They don't really have feelings; their feelings have them. That may be what earlier Christians meant by being "possessed" by a demon. That's why so many of Jesus' miracles are the exorcism of devils. *Most don't take that literally anymore, but the devil is still a powerful*

metaphor [emphasis added], which demands that you take it quite seriously. Everyone has a few devils.[150]

If Christ is "literally everything," then it becomes awkward to explain how Christ could be the father of lies (John 8:44). But if the devil and demons are just metaphors to describe how we go astray, then Rohr can hang on to his "first Incarnation" shtick. It allows him to propose a definition of evil that's as clear as mud: "Whatever stands in the way of a conscious contact between the spiritual and the material in human life, only that is truly evil."[151]

It's not hard to see how modern people could excuse almost any popular evil because it doesn't disrupt "conscious contact" between the spiritual and the material. For Rohr, sin is just another word for "addiction" or "negativity" instead of being, as St. Thomas Aquinas says, "an utterance, a deed, or a desire contrary to the eternal law" (ST I–II. A.71, Q.6).

Because sin is just our own negativity, and Rohr says that "humans are punished *by* their sins more than *for* their sins" (emphasis in the original), it follows that atonement and hell have no place in God's creation. For example, in a review of Mel Gibson's 2004 film *The Passion of the Christ*, Rohr said, "Jesus did not have to die to make God love us, he was paying no debt, he was changing no divine mind. Jesus was only given to change our mind about the nature of God!"[152]

G.K. Chesterton once said, "The whole truth is generally the ally of virtue; a half-truth is always the ally of some vice." Richard Rohr is full of half-truths. He's right that Jesus didn't die to make God love us because God sent his Son to die for our sins precisely because he loved us (John 3:16). But the Crucifixion did affect God, which is why the *Catechism* says, "Jesus atoned for our faults and made satisfaction for our sins to the Father" (615).

However, from Rohr's perspective, Christ's sacrifice doesn't save us from hell because "hell and Christ cannot coexist. . . . We must see Jesus as triumphing over hell and emptying it out."[153] He also says, "Paul never once talks about our notion of hell!" even though 2 Thessalonians 1:9 says of "those who do not obey the gospel of our Lord Jesus" that "these will suffer the punishment of eternal destruction, separated from the presence of the Lord and from the glory of his might."[154] (I wonder if Rohr doubts that 2 Thessalonians is inspired Scripture.)

In closing, what makes Rohr's work so dangerous is not the rigor of his arguments. In many cases, a mere citation from Scripture or the *Catechism* refutes them. What makes them dangerous is their ethereal quality. When Rohr's "theological doozies" are peppered among scores of pages that consist of New Age self-help talk, a reader is lulled into thinking he is becoming a more mystical Christian.

In June of 2022, the pope had an audience with Rohr and allegedly told him, "I want you to keep doing what you're doing, keep teaching what you're teaching."[155] Although the pope is infallible when he teaches "*ex cathedra*," he isn't perfect. The pope may find Fr. Rohr's mysticism personally helpful (for reasons that escape me), but he has failed to see how endorsing Rohr can harm those with weaker faiths, whose interactions with his works can lead them away from the true "Universal Christ."

11

THE RELIABILITY OF THE BIBLE

In September of 2021, I received several emails from concerned Catholics about a video from Fr. Casey Cole, a popular Franciscan priest on YouTube. Some of these Catholics were having a genuine crisis of faith due to his video, which confused me because, although I don't always agree with Cole, his content is rarely sensational.

In this particular video, Cole critiqued what he considered an error in the popular television series *The Chosen*. Specifically, it was a scene depicting the apostles writing down Jesus' words and deeds on notepads immediately after the event took place. Though it was possible in the first century to take notes on pads made of beeswax, I agree with Cole that this probably didn't happen.

If that had been the extent of his critique, I would have had no comment. But then Cole proceeded to subtly undercut the historical nature of the Gospels through comments like these:

The disciples weren't reporters. They didn't think with modern conceptions of history and story-telling like we do, concerned with capturing the facts exactly as they happened. The people who wrote the Gospels, whoever they were and whenever they did it, were theologians. They were writers. They were people not unlike the creators of *The Chosen*, writing years after the fact, with the benefit of lived experience and community reflection, as a means of capturing the significance of Jesus and salvation.[156]

As the whole video makes clear, Cole's intent was to undermine an attitude in *The Chosen* that seems to promote *sola scriptura*, or the belief that our faith is contained in Scripture alone. The deposit of faith was instead given to us in Sacred Scripture and Sacred Tradition, which exists in the life of the Church. But what Cole ended up doing for many of his listeners was to sow seeds of doubt about the historical nature of the Gospels.

Theology, History, or Both?

Cole's assertion that the Evangelists were "theologians, not historians" is inconsistent because, although the Evangelists weren't like modern *historians*, they also weren't like modern *theologians*. They didn't create systematic theologies about things like the Trinity and the Incarnation. They weren't even like theologians of the early Church, who explored allegories and deeper spiritual themes in the life of Jesus. Instead, the Gospel authors practiced both a more ancient form of theology *and* a more ancient form of history. Scholars like Richard Burridge have shown that the Gospels belong to a genre called *bioi*, or what we would call *ancient biography*.[157]

I agree with Cole that the authors of the Gospels did not act like journalists or even modern historians. They didn't intend to record Jesus' life as if it were a deposition in a courtroom. The early second-century Church Father Papias, who knew people who knew the apostles, said for example that

> Mark, having become the interpreter of Peter, wrote down accurately whatsoever he remembered. It was not, however, in exact order that he related the sayings or deeds of Christ. For he neither heard the Lord nor accompanied him. But afterward, as I said, he accompanied Peter, who accommodated his instructions to the necessities [of his hearers], but with no intention of giving a regular narrative of the Lord's sayings.[158]

Ancient biographies don't record a person's life in strict chronological order, nor do they record it in equal intervals from beginning to end. Instead, *bioi* record the aspects of someone's life that were most edifying for their audience. Cole is correct that the Evangelists focused on the *significance* of Jesus' mission, but they did so by recording the historical episodes of Jesus' life that were the most significant. That's why the Evangelists do not record the nearly thirty years of Jesus' life between his birth and the beginning of his public ministry (except for when he was found in the Temple when he was twelve years old).

In his video, Cole never says the Evangelists were historians of any kind (ancient or modern), and the whole video implies that you can do theology, or you can do history, but you can't do both. But this simply isn't the case, as biblical scholar I. Howard Marshall makes in his study of the Gospel of Luke, when he says, "Luke can be properly appreciated as a theologian only when it is recognized that he is also an historian."[159]

It's true that we should not treat the Gospels as if they were simply transcripts of what happened in Jesus' life because that's not how ancient historians and biographers operated. Specifically, they recorded the gist of what the person said without necessarily preserving every single exact word. The ancient Greek historian Thucydides said he recorded history in this way, declaring, "My habit has been to make the speakers say what was in my opinion demanded of them by the various occasions, of course adhering as closely as possible to the general sense of what they really said."[160]

We can see an example of this at Jesus' baptism, since Mark and Luke record the Father telling Jesus, "You are my beloved Son; with you I am well pleased," whereas Matthew records the Father saying, "This is my beloved Son, with whom I am well pleased." But there is no contradiction, since all three writers are asserting the same truth—that Jesus is God's Son—but they do so in different ways.

Even if they use different words to communicate the same truth, the Gospel authors didn't fabricate this event or treat the story of Jesus being baptized as some mere theological allegory. The story has theological significance precisely because it is historical in nature, or it really happened even if the authors vary the small, secondary details associated with the event. The *Catechism* puts it this way:

> The sacred authors, in writing the four Gospels, selected certain of the many elements which had been handed on, either orally or already in written form; others they synthesized or explained with an eye to the situation of the churches, the while sustaining the form of preaching, but always in such a fashion that they have told us the honest truth about Jesus (126).

The Church's "Official" Bible?

Cole also undermined the trustworthiness of the Gospels when he spoke of "the people who wrote the Gospels, whoever they were and whenever they did it" and asserting that it is "pretty well agreed upon" that the Gospels were written sixty to seventy years after the Resurrection.

The Church has no teaching concerning which decade in the first century the Gospels were written, but it does teach that they come from this apostolic period. It also teaches that the Gospels were written by the apostles or those who knew them (such as Mark and Luke), so we could hold that the Gospels of Matthew and John were written by one of their disciples in their name. However, it is reckless to imply that the Gospels were written by some creative storytellers, and we have no idea "whoever they were." This can especially be seen in this comment from Cole:

> We are not reading the literal, eye-witness accounts of people who were there—we are reading the reflections of faith communities, years after the fact, trying to convince others of Good News. . . . [These are] highly symbolic, artfully crafted, works of theology and literature.[161]

How do we know that these people didn't artfully craft a highly symbolic work of *fiction* about Jesus unless we have good evidence of their reliable connections to the apostles?

That's why, in reply to Cole, I laid out the evidence for the Evangelists having direct connections to the apostles and the evidence against the standard view among academics that the Gospels were written after the year A.D. 70. I also pointed out that many of these scholars believe that the Gospels were written after this time period because they contain Jesus' prediction of Jerusalem's destruction. Those scholars assume that this detail must have been added after the fact by early Christians and could not be a genuine prophecy, which reveals many of their naturalistic assumptions.

After receiving criticism for his video, Cole published the following tweet:

> For what it's worth, the introduction of the Gospel of Matthew in the NAB, the translation commissioned by the bishops of the United States, states that Matthew's Gospel was written after 70 AD. Please don't @ me for taking the position of the Church.[162]

The New American Bible (NAB) is the only translation the U.S. bishops have approved for use in the liturgy, but Catholics are free to read and study any Bible and are free to use other translations in non-liturgical religious work like Bible studies. What's more concerning is that Cole assumed that all of the statements in the notes of the New American Bible represent Church teaching.

The bishops' endorsement of the text's use in liturgy does not constitute an endorsement of everything in the study notes, especially as "the position of the Church." The notes even distance themselves from these positions, which can be seen in their use of qualifying statements. For example, concerning the Gospel of Matthew being written by the apostle Matthew, the introduction in the NAB says, "The [position] now favored by the majority of scholars is the following" and proceeds to lay out the view that Matthew was not written by the apostle Matthew.

The notes make it clear that some of what they present regarding authorship and dating of Scripture is just a summary of what is popular in modern biblical studies. A Catholic can accept these findings without giving up the inspiration of

Scripture. He can also reject these findings and accept a more traditional view on the human origin of the scriptures. Pope Francis even said during the hundredth anniversary of the only Catholic university in the Holy Land that the "study, meditation, and reflection on the Bible and biblical texts should be at the heart of the Church, God's holy and faithful people. Outside the body of the Church, these studies are useless."[163]

We can wonder why the U.S. bishops haven't taken advice like this, given the whoppers that can be found in the NAB's study notes, which go beyond run-of-the-mill academic skepticism and venture into heretical waters.

Failure in Footnotes

The Magisterium gives biblical scholars significant leeway in interpreting biblical passages and has infallibly defined the meaning of only a handful of passages in Scripture, such as John 3:5 being a reference to water baptism. However, the Church's teachings on doctrine serve as helpful guardrails to keep biblical scholars from driving off a theological cliff . . . which unfortunately happens on occasion in the New American Bible. Consider the following note on Matthew 16, which says of Jesus' prediction of his death,

> Neither this nor the two later Passion predictions (Matt. 17:22–23, 20:17–19) can be taken as sayings that, as they stand, go back to Jesus himself. However, it is probable that he foresaw that his mission would entail suffering and perhaps death, but was confident that he would ultimately be vindicated by God.

Aside from the problematic assertion that Jesus never uttered these predictions, the Church does not teach that it was "probable" that Jesus knew he would be crucified. It teaches that Jesus had *certain* knowledge of this because it was part of the divine plan of salvation. The *Catechism* quotes Acts 4:27, where Peter reveals that Christ's death at the hands of Roman and Jewish authorities was a part of God's providence:

> When therefore he establishes his eternal plan of "predestination," he includes in it each person's free response to his grace: "In this city, in fact, both Herod and Pontius Pilate, with the Gentiles and the peoples of Israel, gathered together against your holy servant Jesus, whom you anointed, to do whatever your hand and your plan had predestined to take place." For the sake of accomplishing his plan of salvation, God permitted the acts that flowed from their blindness (600).

And in paragraph 474, the *Catechism* affirms that because Jesus is fully divine, he was fully aware of these divine plans: "Jesus did not lack knowledge of his saving mission until he rose from the dead. Instead, Christ enjoyed in his human knowledge the fullness of understanding of the eternal plans he had come to reveal."

This also relates to the NAB's claim that, "as a result of the descent of the Spirit upon him at his baptism (Luke 3:21–22), Jesus is now equipped to overcome the devil." This implies that Jesus was not equipped to overcome the devil prior to his baptism, which is false, given Christ's fully divine, impeccable nature. It also stands in tension with the *Catechism*'s teaching about Christ being "anointed by the Father's Spirit since his incarnation" (727) and this not being reducible to the Spirit's descent at his baptism.

In some cases, revisions done out of liberal biases make the text more off-putting. This can be seen in 1 Corinthians

6:9–10, which contains a list of vices that Paul says will prevent someone from entering into the kingdom of heaven. Two of these are, in Greek, being a *malakoi* and an *arsenokoitai*. In Greek, they literally mean "soft-one" and "man-bedder," respectively, and the Revised Standard Version (RSV) of the Bible translates them together as "homosexuals," though it includes a note saying that what Paul condemns here is homosexual behavior, not merely having same-sex attraction. The NAB, on the other hand, translates *malakoi* as "boy prostitutes" and *arsenokoitai* as "sodomites." In an explanatory note, it says,

> The Greek word translated as "boy prostitutes" may re-fer to *catamites*, i.e., boys or young men who were kept for purposes of prostitution, a practice not uncommon in the Greco-Roman world. In Greek mythology this was the function of Ganymede, the "cupbearer of the gods," whose Latin name was Catamitus. The term translated "sodomites" refers to adult males who indulged in homo-sexual practices with such boys.

It's common among liberal scholars to say that St. Paul con-demned not modern same-sex relationships, but only ancient acts of pederasty or prostitution with young boys. The problem with this interpretation is that Paul would be saying the boys who are victims of sex-trafficking (euphemistically said to be "kept" for sexual acts) will suffer the same eternal fate as their rapists. The alternative translation that sees the *malakoi* and *arse-nokoitai* as the "passive" (anal/oral recipient) and "active" (ejac-ulatory) roles in adult same-sex relationships makes more sense of the grammar, vocabulary, and context of the passage.

I could go on and on with other examples, but the lesson to take away from the NAB's notes and Fr. Cole's commentary is this: always compare biblical commentary to what the Church actually teaches. This is especially the case with the Gospels, since the Church gives a special pre-eminence to these books that describe the life of our Savior, Jesus Christ.

The Christian faith is not a mere message of hope untethered to historical realities. Our hope comes from a God who entered into human history and forever changed it. The *Catechism* puts this point well when it says,

> The Church holds firmly that the four Gospels, "whose historicity she unhesitatingly affirms, faithfully hand on what Jesus, the Son of God, while he lived among men, really did and taught for their eternal salvation, until the day when he was taken up" (126).

12

THE EUCHARIST

After Fr. James Martin, probably one of the best-known Jesuits in America is Fr. Thomas Reese, a man who is no stranger to controversy.

In 1990, Reese oversaw a symposium (later published as a book) that was highly critical of the impending universal *Catechism of the Catholic Church*, in spite of the fact that the document had been released only for the bishops to review. Contributors to Reese's book included Elizabeth Johnson (the dissenting feminist theologian we met in chapter nine), who said the *Catechism* read Scripture in "a fundamentalist way," and Bishop Raymond Lucker, who called it "oppressively sexist."[164]

During this time, Reese was an associate editor of *America* and then served as its editor-in-chief from 1998 until the election of Pope Benedict XVI in 2005. During his tenure, *America* became notorious for publishing articles that undermined Church teaching. This included arguments that "explored" defenses of condoms and a U.S. congressman's criticism of the Church's practice of withholding Communion from politicians who support legal abortion. Pressure from the Congregation for the Doctrine of the Faith led to

Reese being asked to resign in 2005, shortly before Cardinal Ratzinger (the CDF's prefect) became pope.

In articles published since his resignation, Reese has criticized the bishops for their support of politicians who helped overturn *Roe v. Wade*, called climate activist Greta Thunberg a "prophet for Advent," complained about Pope Francis's encyclical *Fratelli Tutti* (All rothers) having a seemingly sexist title, and referred to defenders of contraception and abortion as "those who promote women's rights."[165]

His most eyebrow-raising articles, however, are 2019 and 2023 pieces on the Eucharist. They exemplify a worrying trend among some theologians to move the Eucharist away from being "the source and summit" of our faith (CCC 1324) and reducing it to just another ritual to remind us of our mission to pursue "social justice."

Perpetual Adoration Pushback

In his 2019 article, Reese comments on a recent Pew forum showing that 70 percent of self-identified Catholics think Christ is only symbolically present in the Eucharist. Reese calls this a "failure of catechetics" but goes on to complain about what he considers the real problem: Catholics who focus *too much* on Christ's real presence in the Eucharist.

> The Mass is not about adoring Jesus or even praying to Jesus. . . . The Mass is more about us becoming the body of Christ than it is about the bread becoming the body of Christ. . . . The Eucharist is about making us more Christ-like so that we can continue his mission of establishing the kingdom of God, of bringing justice and peace to the world.[166]

Instead of stamping IHS (the first three letters in the Greek spelling of Jesus' name, *Iesous*) on the eucharistic hosts, it seems Reese would have a us stamp "SJW," or "social justice warrior." In all seriousness, the real problem with Reese's argument is that it creates a false dilemma: either we adore Christ in the Eucharist at Mass or we see the Eucharist as the means to grow in holiness like Christ.

Where Reese has issues with eucharistic piety, the late Fr. Richard McBrien had issues with eucharistic practice. In 2009, McBrien claimed that "the Mass itself provides all that a Catholic needs sacramentally and spiritually. Eucharistic adoration, perpetual or not, is a doctrinal, theological, and spiritual step backward, not forward."[167] This is par for the course for McBrien, whose book *Catholicism* was criticized by the USCCB because it "gives very little weight to the teaching of the Magisterium" and on several moral issues it "regards the 'official Church position' as simply in error."[168]

However, any spiritually mature Catholic will tell you that the latter is impossible without the former. When the wonder of adoration is lost, even during Mass, the liturgy becomes just another empty ritual. Indeed, it's mind-boggling that some liberal Catholics claim perpetual adoration *diverts* people from the Mass since those who are most likely to attend weekly and even daily Mass are those who consistently practice eucharistic adoration.

That's why the *Catechism* says, "In the liturgy of the Mass we express our faith in the real presence of Christ under the species of bread and wine by, among other ways, genuflecting or bowing deeply as a sign of adoration of the Lord" (1378). Pope Francis says silence in the liturgy is necessary because it "disposes us to adore the body and blood of Christ" (*Desiderio Desideravi* 52), and the *Catechism* quotes the following exhortation from John Paul II:

The Church and the world have a great need for eucharistic worship. Jesus awaits us in this sacrament of love. Let us not refuse the time to go to meet him in adoration, in contemplation full of faith, and open to making amends for the serious offenses and crimes of the world. Let our adoration never cease (CCC 1380).

Transcending Transubstantiation

Reese followed up his 2019 piece with a similarly titled 2023 article, where he says, "Since my critics often accuse me of heresy, before I go further, let me affirm that I believe in the real presence of Christ in the Eucharist. I just don't believe in transubstantiation because I don't believe in prime matter, substantial forms, and accidents that are part of Aristotelian metaphysics."[169]

In the past, Reese has demonstrated ignorance not just of theological jargon, but even of basic terms every priest should know. In one article, he writes, "I usually avoid phrases like 'saving souls,' 'God's grace' and 'transubstantiation' because I am not sure what those words mean."[170] This is like a pilot who doesn't know what *altitude* or *pitch* means—he should either quickly learn these terms or quit so that he doesn't cause tremendous harm to others!

Reese would probably say he doesn't need to know what "transubstantiation" is because it is an awkward import from Aquinas's synthesis of Aristotelian philosophy and not a part of the Faith itself. It's true that the *term* "transubstantiation" is not part of the Faith, but a theological tool to help us understand. Similar terms that do not come from the deposit of faith would include *hypostatic union*, *Trinity*, and even *Bible*. They could be substituted with other words, but the dogmas they represent can't be rejected.

Transubstantiation, moreover, is not a holdover from Aquinas's synthesis of Aristotelian philosophy. It is a Latin term that was used two hundred years before Aquinas in the writings of Bishop Hildebert of Tours and among dissenting theologians like Berengar of Tours, who objected to the term. The Fourth Lateran Council used the term ten years before Aquinas was born when it spoke of "the bread being transubstantiated into the body by the divine power and the wine into the blood."

Fr. McBrien also tiptoes toward the edge of heresy on this topic when he claims,

> The transformation (the medieval word was "transubstantiation") is sacramental, not literal or physical. In other words, the bread and the wine retain the properties of bread and wine. They look like bread and wine and taste like bread and wine, but Catholics (and many other Christians as well) believe that the bread and wine have been sacramentally changed into the body and blood of Christ.[171]

Transubstantiation and *transformation* are not synonyms. During the consecration, the form or appearance of the bread and wine does not change, even though there is a real change in their substance. Pope Paul VI taught in *Mysterium Fidei* that "once the substance or nature of the bread and wine has been changed into the body and blood of Christ, nothing remains of the bread and the wine except for the species—beneath which Christ is present whole and entire in his physical 'reality,' corporeally present, although not in the manner in which bodies are in a place" (46).

In other words, the change that takes place isn't merely "sacramental" in nature. (Lutherans refer to their eucharist as possessing "sacramental union" while denying transubstantiation.) The Council of Trent infallibly defined that one must believe in that "wonderful and unique change of the whole substance of the bread into his body and of the whole substance of the wine into his blood," which is "fittingly" called transubstantiation.[172]

Catholic apologist Jimmy Akin, who has written an entire book on interpreting Church documents, soberly analyzes the peril inherent in Reese's rejection of the term *transubstantiation*:

> The term *transubstantiation* was coined in the 1000s, so it is not part of the deposit of faith and not divinely revealed. Reese would not be a heretic for denying this term. But in rejecting transubstantiation, Reese said that "Christ's presence in the Eucharist is an unexplainable mystery." On its face, that appears to be a doubt of (a refusal to believe) the explanation provided by Trent—that the whole substance of bread and wine are changed into the whole substance of Christ's body and blood. Reese thus should clarify whether he actually accepts this change, which is divinely revealed and was made a dogma by Trent.[173]

The Eucharist and Pro-abortion Politicians

After Joe Biden became the second Catholic U.S. president, the U.S. bishops voted to include a section in their upcoming document on eucharistic coherence to address the problem of dissenting Catholic politicians.

Contrary to what some liberal critics claim, the bishops never proposed a national policy barring all pro-abortion politicians from the Eucharist. They proposed only that every bishop be free to invoke canon 915, which says that those who are "obstinately persevering in manifest grave sin" should not be admitted to Holy Communion. But some liberal Catholics say bishops should *never* withhold the Eucharist to pro-abortion politicians because doing so "weaponizes the Eucharist" and causes scandal in its own right. Michael Sean Winters says, "It is foolish to think that Biden going to Communion will confuse anyone about what the Church teaches regarding the evil of abortion. Is there anyone who does not know the Church's position? No. Why then, this crusade?"[174]

The answer is that most people (and even most Catholics) have only a superficial knowledge of Church teaching.

Yes, many people identify Catholicism with being "against abortion," but if they also see a politician hailed for "being a faithful Catholic" while voting to keep abortion legal, then they might think there is nothing wrong with what he's doing, or at least that it couldn't be *that bad*. "Abortion may be something distasteful to personally oppose, but it's not murder," they think. But they would be mistaken, since John Paul II said there is a "grave and clear obligation to oppose" laws promoting euthanasia and abortion (*Evangelium Vitae* 73). The Congregation for the Doctrine of the Faith said, "A well-formed Christian conscience does not permit one to vote for a political program or an individual law which contradicts the fundamental contents of faith and morals."[175]

Another argument is that politicians who support legal abortion haven't committed a grave sin since they have not performed an abortion or referred any individual woman to have an abortion. These kinds of arguments were raised when Archbishop Salvatore Cordileone of San Francisco barred speaker of the House Nancy Pelosi from receiving Communion. Cordileone said the action had to be taken "after numerous attempts to speak with her to help her understand the grave evil she is perpetrating, the scandal she is causing and the danger to her own soul she is risking."[176]

In response, liberal Catholics said that (to their knowledge) Pelosi had never paid for an abortion or counseled a woman to have an abortion. Therefore, she could not be violating the Church's teachings on abortion. Similarly with Biden, Winters said,

> Biden is not performing abortions and he has never, to my knowledge, questioned the Church's teaching on abortion. . . . If he is wrong—and I think he is—he is wrong about how to properly relate a Catholic's necessary commitment to the protection of all human life with the political realities he faces. My Catholic friends who are Republican face the exact same kind of difficulty on other issues.[177]

This is not a case of Biden or Pelosi allowing exceptions for abortion in order to navigate the political realities of a pluralistic society. Church teaching already allows Catholic politicians to tolerate less than ideal laws in order to obtain the most feasible defense of human life. John Paul II made this clear in *Evangelium Vitae*: "When it is not possible to overturn or completely abrogate a pro-abortion law, an elected official, whose absolute personal opposition to procured abortion was well known, could licitly support proposals aimed at limiting the harm done by such a law" (73).

This is also not a case of a politician merely espousing pro-abortion rhetoric ("I support the right to choose!"). Instead, Biden has sought to *expand* abortion law, and after the *Dobbs v. Jackson* decision, he encouraged Congress to pass a law codifying *Roe v. Wade* at the federal level. Speaker Pelosi shared a similar goal and has also compounded the sin of scandal by appearing on national television programs and confusing people about Church teaching on abortion by citing Augustine's and Aquinas's views on ensoulment, even though both Doctors of the Church held abortion to be gravely evil.

The claim that pro-abortion politicians don't "violate Church teaching" is as absurd as saying that a Catholic politician who passes a federal ban on "anti-lynching laws" or "racial integration" doesn't sin because he isn't personally committing acts of racist evil. He is still culpable, perhaps of even greater evils, because with the stroke of a pen he has made it possible for evil to spread and impossible for good people to legally stop it.

Weaponizing Rhetoric's Fatal Flaw

This brings us to the biggest weakness of arguments against withholding Communion for pro-abortion politicians: asking its proponents, "Is there *any law* a politician could vote for that is so heinous, so evil, that it would signify that he is manifestly and obstinately persisting in grave sin and should therefore be prohibited from receiving Communion?"

The defender of this argument is in the horns of a dilemma.

If he says voting to support genocide or deport innocent people to death camps are acts that merit the withholding of Communion, we can ask why supporting other instances of homicide like abortion does not. If he bites the bullet and says no legislative action could justify withholding Communion, then he reveals a moral repugnance in his worldview. For example, in May of 2022, I asked Steven Millies on Twitter the following question: a Catholic politician introduces a bill to make it legal for ranchers to use lethal force against illegal immigrants who merely trespass on their property. Should that politician be denied Communion?

His response? "No politician should be denied Communion. That's my bottom line."[178]

This stands in stark contrast to previous Catholic bishops who held civil authorities to account when they violated God's law. In 1962, Archbishop Rummel of New Orleans excommunicated Catholic political figures who opposed racial integration. Liberal Catholics counter this example by saying Rummel excommunicated only politicians who opposed Catholic schools desegregating, not racist politicians in general. Fr. Reese says, "The only thing comparable would be if some Catholics started a movement to insist that Catholic hospitals do abortions."[179] Except that's precisely what Xavier Becerra, the Catholic secretary of Health and Human Services, tried to do until a federal appeals court stopped him in *Franciscan Alliance v. Becerra* (2016).

If trying to force a Catholic hospital to kill children doesn't justify withholding Communion, what does?

My favorite example of holding civil leaders to account is St. Ambrose, who stood up to Emperor Theodosius after he ordered his troops to massacre 7,000 men, women, and children in Thessalonica in response to a riot in the city. In response, Ambrose demanded that the emperor perform a public penance before he could be readmitted to the Church, to which he agreed. At the emperor's funeral, Ambrose said, "He stripped himself of every sign of royalty and bewailed his sin openly in church. He, an emperor, was not ashamed to do the public penance which lesser individuals shrink from, and to the end of his life he never ceased to grieve for his error."[180]

I pray more bishops will follow the example of Ambrose and Cordileone and hold elected leaders accountable for their errors, both for the sake of those they govern and for their own souls, since they will have to account for the evils they enabled when they stand before God on the Day of Judgment.

13

APOLOGETICS

In a 2021 article, Michael Sean Winters claimed that Pope Francis "delivered a strong rebuke to Los Angeles Archbishop José Gómez, Bishop Robert Barron, auxiliary of the same archdiocese, and groups such as 'Catholic Answers' and EWTN in a Dec. 4 speech to the clergy, religious and seminarians of Athens, Greece."[181] Winters admits that Pope Francis didn't actually mention any of these people or groups by name, but he claims that the pope's description of evangelization is markedly different from what "U.S. conservatives" practice.

Other liberal Catholics claim that apologetics is a relic of a bygone era and that its continued use alienates potential converts to the Faith. For example, John Vitek criticized Bishop Barron's desire for a "new apologetics" to engage religious "nones," saying, "Might we better serve today's young people if the Church's 'priority one' were, at least as our starting point, witnessing to the joy of the gospel by inspiring their hearts, engaging their religious imaginations, and honoring their lived experiences through deep and nonjudgmental listening?"[182]

Inspiring, engaging, and listening to non-Catholics are crucial to evangelism. But so are questioning and convincing those same people that the Catholic faith is *true*. And apologetics is one of the best ways to demonstrate this truth, especially when it is done in an engaging way that listens to those it seeks to persuade.

A False Dilemma

Winters claims that coupling apologetics with evangelism is problematic because it presents the Faith "as a series of propositions to which people are expected to give their assent."

There are people who treat the Faith in a reductive way and overlook the importance of having an encounter with Jesus Christ. There are also people who pursue apologetics as part of an obnoxious triumphalism that is concerned only with winning arguments. They are the kind of Catholic Fulton Sheen warned about when he said, "You can win an argument and lose a soul."

But just because apologetics can be done badly doesn't mean we need to get rid of it or "reform it" beyond recognition. People can perform works of mercy like feeding the poor in a patronizing and condescending way that "loses a soul." All of our evangelism should imitate Christ, such as when he graciously refuted opponents like the Pharisees and used those opportunities to call more people to believe in the gospel. Winters then claims,

> You can go to the website of Catholic Answers, or watch almost any show on EWTN and you will find a similar approach to evangelization: we have the answers, and if people were not so easily duped by the evil of the world,

they would recognize that we have the answers, embrace our answers, and submit.[183]

The claim that Catholic Answers (and by implication Catholic apologists in general) demands that non-Catholics "embrace our answers and submit" is a caricature. There's no shortage of apologetic works engaging atheists, Protestants, and even dissenting Catholics that follow Isaiah's call for us to "reason together" (1:18).

It also amazes me that critics of apologetics think that we can *either* joyfully live out the Faith and engage in works of charity *or* engage in apologetics, but we can't do both. Apologetics fall on deaf ears if the person making them is a dour killjoy or if the person hearing them is totally preoccupied with where he will get his next meal.

On the other hand, you can't help someone receive the Faith that is necessary for salvation if you *only* feed him or *only* listen to his opinions and never present the gospel to him. And when you do present the gospel, he might have follow-up questions like "How do we know this wasn't all made up?" or "Why do I need to go to Church if I already believe in Jesus?" And here is where we should practice apologetics in the manner St. Peter recommended: "Reverence Christ as Lord. [And] always be prepared to make a defense to any one who calls you to account for the hope that is in you, yet do it with gentleness and reverence" (1 Pet. 3:15).

Patronizing "Anti-apologetics"

Apologetics is not identical to evangelism. It is possible to share the good news of Jesus Christ and his Church with someone (i.e., evangelize him) without engaging in an "apologetic" or a defense of any particular doctrine. In those cases, evangelism efforts might primarily overcome an emotional or spiritual obstacle to the person being in full communion with Christ and his Church. But in other cases, a person may have intellectual obstacles and may even use those obstacles to camouflage his more emotional objections.

The Protestant pastor Timothy Keller once shared about how a fellow pastor he knew would engage college students who told him they were having doubts about their faith. He spoke to one young man for a while about scientific and historical objections to the Christian faith before asking him, "Whom have you been sleeping with?" The student was shocked and asked in reply, "How did you know?"

Now, there are intellectual objections to Catholicism that constitute a person's primary objection and don't merely disguise emotional objections. For example, a person may say he is emotionally upset about the Church's prohibition on same-sex "marriages," but the root of his emotional turmoil is a firm intellectual conviction that the proposition "homosexual conduct is sinful" is false. This comports with recent studies that show that the biggest reason people give for leaving religion is that they no longer think it is true.[184] In fact, it's condescending to those with serious intellectual objections to say the real obstacle to their conversion is a lack of "inclusive Catholics" who focus on works of charity more than "winning debates."

For example, in June 2021, a Jesuit scholastic tweeted about how Catholics should simply go to LGBT pride parades and pass out water to show their love and support for the LGBT community. Chrissy Stroop, who identifies as a transgender woman, commented on the tweet and recounted how Christians often do this before pride parades. Stroop then offered the following insightful commentary on those who want only to "build a bridge" to the LGBT community but refuse to engage their deepest objections to Catholicism:

> If you're really serious about wanting to be "decent" toward queer people, you ought to save your apologies and your bottled water and stay home. Maybe while there, you could do some reflecting on how there's no such thing as "kinder, gentler" culture warring. It's not "loving" to believe that sexual and gender minorities either shouldn't exist or shouldn't express who we are in loving relationships. Don't come begging us for forgiveness until you've actually changed your harmful views, which you shouldn't hide behind "friendly" rhetoric.[185]

I have evangelized the attendees of LGBT pride parades, and charity and compassion are certainly prerequisites to having a productive conversation—but they are a *means* to communicating the truth of the gospel. They are not the gospel itself.

There are cases where a person's biggest obstacle to accepting the Faith is the wounds inflicted upon him by demeaning or uncharitable Christians. In those cases, a kind heart and cold bottle of water may be helpful. But in other cases, acts of kindness reach an impasse on questions like "What is God's plan for our sexuality?" When that happens, we must engage in apologetic dialogue to challenge the person's worldview and help him find truth and joy in Jesus Christ.

Apologetics Is for "Fundamentalists"?

Perhaps the strangest attack on apologetics I have come across among liberal Catholics can be found in Sean Swain

Martin's 2021 book, *American Pope: Scott Hahn and the Rise of Catholic Fundamentalism.*

In the academic world, the nastiest thing you can call another scholar is the "F-word," or a *fundamentalist.* The word conjures up images of an unthinking zealot who rejects scholarly methods because of his irrational preconceived ideas. One of Martin's evidences that Hahn is indeed a "fundamentalist" is because Hahn is committed to the use of apologetics.

For example, Martin criticizes Hahn for using the RSV's translation of 1 Peter 3:15 ("make a defense to anyone who calls you to account for the hope that is in you") over the NAB's translation ("give an explanation to anyone who asks you for a reason for your hope"). Martin says both verses have "fundamentally different connotations," and the latter is speaking more of sharing how "Christ and the Church have moved in [our] life" rather than engaging in apologetical debates.[186]

But explanations can involve defenses, so the two translations do not have "fundamentally different connotations." The Greek word translated "defense" in the RSV and "explanation" in the NAB is *apologian,* from which we get the word "apologetics." Either English word is an appropriate translation, as can be seen in the NAB's rendering of Philippians 1:16, where Paul says, "I am here for the defense (*apologian*) of the gospel."

Martin also criticizes Hahn's approach to apologetics as one that seeks to "win over" people with "proofs of Christianity." Martin says this approach stands "at tension with the [Catholic] tradition," which is a baffling claim, given the long history of apologetics in spreading the Catholic faith.

The Church's first deacon, St. Stephen, debated people in the synagogue so fiercely that his opponents "could not withstand the wisdom and the Spirit with which he spoke" (Acts 6:10). Paul spent every day in Athens arguing in the marketplace (17:17), and in Ephesus he "argued daily in the hall of Tyrannus. This continued for two years, so that all the residents of Asia heard the word of the Lord, both Jews and Greeks" (19:9–10).

Martin also claims that the patron saint of apologists, Justin Martyr (whom Martin erroneously refers to simply as "Martyr," as if it were a last name) did not try "to win over his interlocutor with proofs of Christianity." I don't know how Martin arrived at this conclusion, given that in Justin's Dialogue with Rabbi Trypho, he uses various proofs to show that Jesus is the Messiah.

As Cardinal Avery Dulles shows in his book *A History of Apologetics*, in the centuries after Justin, we find apologists defending grace against the Pelagians, Christ's divinity against the Arians, and the value of human life against the barbarians. The apologetical enterprise continued into the medieval and modern ages with saints like John of Damascus, Thomas Aquinas, and Francis de Sales engaging Muslim, pagan, and Protestant arguments against Catholicism.

Martin also claims that Hahn's conversion to Catholicism was an example of how apologetics motivates a prideful intellectual self-sufficiency. He says this stands in contrast to someone like Cardinal Henry Newman, who "gave over his prideful belief in his absolute self-sufficiency" and instead turned to "the simple quiet wisdom of a local parish priest."

Except, in Newman's autobiography, he says his doubts went away due to his research on doctrinal development, and not simply an encounter with a humble priest. In 1845, Newman asked Fr. Dominic Berberi to simply receive him into the Church, not for nuggets of quiet wisdom. Newman probably saw in Berberi a kindred spirit, as the priest also had a reputation for arguing for the Faith. But Newman asked him to receive him into the Church because he had already been convinced by his apologetical research that Catholicism is true (which mirrors Hahn's own journey as a convert). Newman writes, "As I advanced [in writing], my difficulties so cleared away that I ceased to speak of 'the Roman Catholics,' and boldly called them Catholics."[187]

A New Apologetic?

Other liberal Catholics understand the value of apologetics but believe that its emphasis on defending the deposit of faith is simply too narrow. Matt Kappadakunnel, a contributor to *Where Peter Is*, affirms apologetics in defense of doctrines like the communion of saints, but he goes on to say that "we should not limit the defense of the Faith to baseline challenges like these, as relevant as they are." Instead, after reflecting upon race issues in the U.S. after the death of George Floyd, Kappadakunnel says, "Our defense of the Faith must include the defense of the *people* who are oppressed," and "it's time for the Catholic apologetics movement to turn their focus to defending black lives."[188]

Kappadakunnel's claims are admirable, but his proposal mirrors the faulty "seamless garment" approach that tries to make every problem people face, from low wages to pollution, a "life issue." Just as turning everything into a "life issue" for pro-lifers to solve dilutes the pro-life movement and hampers its ability to fight abortion and euthanasia, pressing apologetics into the service of every conceivable social justice issue would severely dilute its meaning and impact.

Apologetics, properly speaking, is a branch of theology dedicated to providing a rational defense of the Catholic faith. This includes not just issues of faith, but also moral issues, like abortion, where apologists must make a case for things like the humanity of unborn children. Apologetics would also be appropriate in past (and even some present-day) contexts that rejected the Church's teachings on slavery or antisemitism.

But just because some Catholic apologetical arguments involve contemporary moral issues, that doesn't mean that apologetics should focus on any popular issue people are arguing about.

In cases of racist violence, nearly everyone agrees that an act of evil was committed, and the legal system should punish those responsible. This is similar to how deaths from gun violence are not a "pro-life issue," since everyone agrees that innocent born people have a right not to be gunned down. The finite resources of Catholic apologetics are best used to defend the doctrines of the Faith the world rejects (like the evil nature of abortion and contraception) rather than to affirm truths the world largely accepts (like the evil nature of gun violence and racism).

In fact, in the remaining chapters of this book, we will see that liberal Catholics overstate their case when they demand that Catholics embrace their particular solutions to social problems like racism, gun violence, and climate change.

14

RACISM

On June 19, 2020, in the aftermath of protests and riots un-
folding across the country after the killing of George Floyd,
Catholic Charities of Eastern Washington president Rob
McCann posted on the group's YouTube channel a truly
bizarre statement. He said the controversies surrounding
Floyd's death

> made me realize some important things about my own
> life that maybe I always knew but never truly embraced
> with enough blunt truth. I am a racist. That's the hard
> truth. I am a racist. How could I not be as a white person
> living in America, where every institution is geared to
> advantage people who look like me? It's seemingly im-
> possible for me to be anything other than a racist.

McCann went on to say that Catholic Charities and even
the Catholic Church itself are racist. He declared, "How
could they not be? Our Catholic faith tradition is built on
the premise that a baby, born in a manger, in the Middle
East, was a white baby. So how can we be surprised to know
that we must still fight against racism?"[189]

Normally, if a Catholic ministry leader admitted to habitually engaging in a grave evil like racism, you'd expect him to resign in disgrace or at least be terminated by the ministry's board of directors. If he thought his employer and his church were racist, then you'd expect him to leave both of those racist institutions. But the times in which we live are anything but normal. According to liberal academics and their Catholic allies, what McCann did was what every white person should do: admit to being racist, since all white people are racist.

Defining "Racism"

Whereas Catholics and non-Catholics often disagree on controversial issues like abortion, they usually agree that racism is evil. The problem is that some liberal Catholics have distorted the Church's teaching on racism in order to join it to a false and dehumanizing ideology that calls itself "anti-racist" but is in fact one of the most pervasive examples of racism alive today.

Anti-racists claim that white people are racist by nature and prone to other forms of violence. A festival in Paris demanded that whites be excluded from "black only spaces." A Michigan school trustee said online that "whiteness is so evil" and advised a hiker to worry more about white people than dangerous animals.[190] A diversity training specialist at Coca-Cola instructed attendees to be "less white."[191] Robin DiAngelo says in her bestselling book *White Fragility* that a white person's mere objection to being called racist is further evidence of his racism.[192]

There are many examples of whites being racist toward non-white people, but the point that should be taken from any act of racism is that *no race* should be degraded or treated as being less valuable than other races. The *Catechism* teaches that racism is evil because it contradicts the equal dignity *every* human being possesses:

> Created in the image of the one God and equally endowed with rational souls, all men have the same nature and the same origin. . . . The equality of men rests essentially on their dignity as persons and the rights that flow from it: every form of social or cultural discrimination in fundamental personal rights on the grounds of sex, race, color, social conditions, language, or religion must be curbed and eradicated as incompatible with God's design (1934-1935).

One of the Church's boldest condemnations of racism in the modern world came in 1937, when Pope Pius XI issued the encyclical *Mit brennender Sorge* (With Deep Anxiety). The first encyclical written in German, it was smuggled into Nazi Germany, and it forcefully condemned the racist ideology of the Nazi state:

> Whoever exalts race, or the people, or the State, or a particular form of State, or the depositories of power, or any other fundamental value of the human community—however necessary and honorable be their function in worldly things—whoever raises these notions above their standard value and divinizes them to an idolatrous level, distorts and perverts an order of the world planned and created by God; he is far from the true faith in God and from the concept of life which that faith upholds (8).

Traditionally, racism was understood as the sinful attitude that some human beings have less intrinsic dignity than other human beings, and so it is acceptable to marginalize, mistreat, enslave, or even kill members of this "inferior" group. Today, however, definitions of racism go far beyond this commonsense understanding.

Instead of focusing on internal attitudes that denigrate fellow human beings, modern "anti-racists" (as they call themselves) focus on external disparities among racial groups. If a non-white race is underrepresented in a good thing (like college attendance rates) or overrepresented in a bad thing (like incarceration rates), then the only explanation for this discrepancy is racism.

One difficulty in evaluating modern anti-racist literature is that it often relies on circular definitions. For example, in his book *How to Be an Anti-racist*, Ibram X. Kendi defines racism as "a powerful collection of racist policies that lead to racial inequity and are substantiated by racist ideas."[193] The addition of the word "racist" makes the definition useless, but it keeps Kendi from having to assume that all disparities are racist.

Fr. Dan Horan says in his book *A White Catholic's Guide to Racism and Privilege* that racism "is a culture that justifies inequality and disparity between people identified according to their perceived race."[194] But under this definition, historically black colleges that only or primarily admit black applicants would be racist, since they would have a disparity in white students. Likewise, schools that treat Asian applicants unequally in order not to have too many Asians attend would be guilty of racism. (This actually is racist, but since the policy favors the admission of non-white people, liberals often think it is not racist.)

In fact, Fr. Horan denies that "reverse racism" is even possible. He claims that whereas non-whites can be guilty of prejudice, only whites can be racist, since their prejudice is reinforced by social systems of racism. This leads to the following, qualified definition: "Racism is any prejudice against someone because of their race, *when those views are reinforced by systems of power.*" Fr. Horan also cites Fr. Bryan Massingale, who claims, "The only reason for the persistence of racism is because white people benefit from it."[195]

Under this view, racism is not merely a disparity among racial groups; it is any disparity that benefits white people, because white people are uniquely able to be racist. Ironically, this approach to racism is itself racist because it treats non-whites as being incapable of doing something whites can do: be racist.

Irony aside, this framework is spiritually harmful because it ignores racism among non-whites, of which non-whites, too, need to repent. In some cases, this approach actively encourages non-whites to be racist through "diversity, equity, and inclusion" seminars that tell attendees that "all white people are racist." It's no wonder that one study profiled in the *Harvard Business Review* found that mandatory diversity training programs led to less racial diversity in the workplace. It noted how "people often respond to compulsory courses with anger and resistance—and many participants actually report more animosity toward other groups afterward."[196]

That modern "anti-racism" movements contradict the Church's traditional desire for racial harmony can be seen in their embrace of anti-racist discrimination. Kendi says, "The only remedy to racist discrimination is anti-racist discrimination. The only remedy to past discrimination is present discrimination. The only remedy to present discrimination is future discrimination."[197]

This is incompatible with a faith that preaches, as St. Paul did, that we may not do evil that good may come of it (Rom. 3:8) and that "there is neither Jew nor Greek, there is neither slave nor free, there is neither male nor female; for you are all one in Christ Jesus" (Gal. 3:28).

Racism and Capitalist Systems

The anti-racist approach is also problematic because it says that people can oppose racism only if they oppose capitalism, since capitalism is one of the alleged causes of systemic racism. Olga M. Segura argues in her book *Birth of a Movement: Black Lives Matter and the Catholic Church* that racism is not the result of individual immoral choices. Instead, it is an inevitable byproduct of capitalism. As a result, she says the Church "must embrace" anti-capitalism. A sympathetic review of her book in *America* magazine says,

> Segura identifies capitalism as the social factor that cements racism into daily life in the United States. Racism is not an accident perpetrated by intentional bigots or an obsolete method of structuring society: it is a founding tenet of our country, encoded into the design of our neighborhoods, financial systems, and workforce.[198]

But previous popes have said that capitalism (or free market economies), though capable of facilitating evil acts, is itself evil. In *Centesimus annus* (The Hundredth Year), John Paul II supported capitalist economies that recognize "the fundamental and positive role of business, the market, private property, and the resulting responsibility for the means of production" (42). Pope Francis has been extremely critical of abuses within market economies, but, as he writes in his 2023 book *El Pastor,* "I do not condemn capitalism in the way some attribute to me."[199] He even wrote in *Laudato Si* (Praised Be): "Business is a noble vocation directed to producing wealth and improving the world" (129).

None of what I've argued should be construed to mean that social systems are without sin. The *Catechism* teaches that sinful acts can perpetuate harm through sinful social structures: "Sins give rise to social situations and institutions that are contrary to the divine goodness. 'Structures of sin' are the expression and effect of personal sins. They lead their victims to do evil in their turn. In an analogous sense, they constitute a 'social sin'" (1869).

The damaging effect of sinful behavior can exist long after society has rejected that sinful behavior, such as how slavery and racial segregation made the descendants of black Americans worse off. But modern "anti-racism" ideologies minimize or even ignore the personal aspects of the sin of racism. They often identify it with the social structures of sin isolated from any personal responsibility. Indeed, even one of Kendi's children's books on anti-racism simply says, "People aren't the problem—policies are."[200]

In contrast, Pope St. John Paul II tells us that this approach (which, he says, is popular with non-Christians) leads to the erroneous belief that "practically every sin is a social sin, in the sense that blame for it is to be placed not so much on the moral conscience of an individual, but rather on some vague entity or anonymous collectivity such as the situation, the system, society, structures, or institutions" (*Reconciliatio et Paenitentia* 16). The Pontifical Commission for Peace and Justice likewise said, "Racial prejudice, which denies the equal dignity of all the members of the human family and blasphemes the Creator, can only be eradicated by going to its roots, where it is formed: in the human heart."[201]

Ally for Me, but Not for Thee

Finally, one of the most galling examples of hypocrisy among liberal Catholics is that they rightly condemn Catholics who discriminate against non-white people but tolerate Catholics who discriminate against people "of the womb," or the unborn.

Consider how liberal Catholics have incessantly criticized Bishop Robert Barron's partnerships with Jordan Peterson because they claim that Peterson is a bigoted misogynist.[202] Any truths the non-Catholic Peterson might share simply don't outweigh his other views, which they find odious. However, these same people have a near infinite amount of tolerance for Catholic anti-racism advocates who openly reject important Catholic doctrine.

For example, Amanda Gorman, a young black Catholic poet, was given fawning coverage in outlets like *America*.[203] Yet, when the Catholic News Agency pointed out that just two years earlier, Gorman had recited a pro-abortion poem at Harvard that called abortion "liberating," D.W. Lafferty, a former contributor to *Where Peter Is*, tersely replied, "Do we have to sit through four years of CNA pointing out how everyone is connected to abortion somehow?"[204] (I'm sure Lafferty wouldn't be amused if a conservative Catholic told him, "How long do we have to listen to you point out how everyone is racist?")

Similarly, in a review of Olga Segura's book *Birth of a Movement: Black Lives Matter and the Catholic Church*, *Where Peter Is* contributor Matt Kappadakunnel only says, "There are certain ideas presented in the book that are not in alignment with Church teaching, such as on gender theory."[205]

That's putting it lightly.

Segura says the Catholic position on the nature of men and women is "not Christianity" and says pro-abortion activists like Tarana Burke are more Catholic than the bishops. She even says, "Black Lives Matter presents a more nuanced and intersectional understanding of reproductive justice than the Catholic Church," even though BLM cooperates with groups that advocate for unrestricted access to abortion.[206]

This brings us to the matter of whether Catholics must (or even should) support BLM, or other organizations like it.

Good Idea, Questionable Organization

As I noted in chapter two, Bishop Robert McManus of Worcester, Massachusetts rescinded a Jesuit middle school's Catholic status after it refused to stop flying an LGBT pride flag and a BLM flag on campus. McManus said the Church "stands unequivocally" behind the phrase "black lives matter" but added that BLM "promotes a platform that directly contradicts Catholic social teaching." This includes pages on the group's website that link anti-racism efforts with promoting transgender ideology, abortion, and the breakdown of the nuclear family. McManus even said, "Flags bearing the words 'end racism' and 'we are all God's children' would be far more appropriate for a Catholic school."[207]

This wasn't good enough for the liberal mob. (It never is.) Bishop McManus was pilloried as a bigoted racist. In fact, some Catholics have said that in order truly to be anti-racist, Catholics *must* support the organization called Black Lives Matter.

Olga Segura says in *America* magazine that Catholics "must explicitly stand with our brothers and sisters marching and chanting that Black Lives Matter."[208] Jamie Manson, the president of Catholics for Choice, writes in the *National Catholic Reporter*, "I am angry that Catholic leaders refused to say Black Lives Matter, and that many instead used its cowardly counterpart All Lives Matter." (Of course, Manson's support for abortion shows that she certainly does not believe that "all lives matter.")[209]

The BLM movement gained national notoriety after the 2014 shooting of Michael Brown. Through a series of protests and media appearances, the movement established in the public consciousness the idea that Michael Brown was murdered in cold blood by a police officer while Brown was trying to surrender. Protesters and liberal pundits liked to chant in imitation of Brown's alleged last words, "Hands up, don't shoot!"

However, an extensive investigation conducted by the Obama-era Justice Department involving over a hundred witnesses concluded that Brown never said this, but instead charged at the officer, who fired his service weapon in self-defense.[210] Likewise, in the case of George Floyd, the Minnesota attorney general declined to charge officer Derek Chauvin with a hate crime for Floyd's killing, citing a lack of evidence of a racial motivation.[211]

Catholics must believe that "black lives matter" just as they believe that the life of every human being matters. But that doesn't mean they must support BLM as a political movement or any other movement that has an undeniably true slogan as its official name. In fact, there are prudent reasons for a Catholic *not* to support such a movement.

First, BLM's protests during the summer of 2020 often became violent riots. Alessandra Harris, a contributor for *America* magazine, claims that "97.7 percent of protests during 2020 were peaceful with no injuries reported among participants, bystanders, or police. Only 3.7 percent resulted in property damage or vandalism. Police were injured in 1 percent of the protests."[212] This leaves out more pertinent details, like the fact that about a dozen people were killed and there was over a billion dollars in property damage in these 2020 protests, making them the costliest U.S. civil disorder in history.[213]

Second, since BLM's founding in 2013, race relations have gotten worse. Since the 1990s, Gallup polling had indicated that a majority of whites (70 percent) and blacks (60 percent) believed that race relations in America were good. This opinion began to decline after 2013, and by 2021, the majority of whites (57 percent) and blacks (67 percent) *denied* that race relations are good.

One explanation for this trend is that the media's constant pronouncement that America is "systemically racist" has distorted people's perceptions of reality. The same thing occurs when people mistakenly think violent crime has increased in the past few decades, when it is only *news coverage* of violent crimes that has increased, since violent crime rates have decreased from record highs in the 1990s. And the same thing can be seen in the media's coverage of specific crimes (like the shooting of Michael Brown) as well as their coverage of police violence in general.

Finally, legitimate concerns have been raised about the organization's use of donor funds. Tens of millions of dollars have remained in the organization's bank accounts, and other funds were spent on luxuries like a six-million-dollar southern California mansion, described as a place where BLM leaders can "plan and organize outside of the confines of white supremacy." (The mansion is located in Studio City, an affluent Los Angeles neighborhood where only 4 percent of the population is black.)[214]

No one knows the prominence BLM will hold in future debates over racial equality in America, but there will certainly be other social justice organizations that capture the public's imagination and demand support from faithful Catholics. The lesson from BLM is that Catholics should exercise prudence when choosing to support organizations committed to promoting the common good. A catchy name or charismatic leader can mask serious underlying problems, or even beliefs that contradict the Catholic faith.

St. Paul's advice regarding spiritual matters is equally helpful when it comes to deciding which charities or advocacy groups to support: "Test everything, retain what is good" (1 Thess. 5:21).

15

LIBERATION THEOLOGY

In 2020, Brazil's foreign minister, Ernesto Aruajo, got into a Twitter spat with liberation theologian Leonardo Boff, saying,

> When your liberation theology appeared, more than 90 percent of Brazilians were Catholic. Today they're only 50 percent and [they keep] going down. Brazilians—especially the poor—rejected your theo-Marxism and ran to the Evangelical churches, where they can praise Jesus Christ.[215]

Some people think liberation theology is a forgotten relic of 1970s Latin American culture—but in fact, its disastrous effects persist into the present day. And you can still find liberal Catholics extolling its supposed virtues.

Michael Lee offers a fawning review on the fiftieth anniversary of one of liberation theology's foundational texts, *A Theology of Liberation*, calling it a "powerful" and "prophetic" critique. He also expresses optimism toward liberation theology, saying, "Its death has been declared prematurely far too many times."[216] And the headline of a piece by a

Jesuit priest in *America* melodramatically declares, "Once I discovered liberation theology, I couldn't be Catholic without it."[217]

But upon closer examination, we see that many people cease being Catholic because of the Marxist ideology that is prevalent throughout the works of liberation theology.

What Is Liberation Theology?

Liberation theology was coined by Fr. Gustavo Gutierrez in 1971 and later expanded upon in his book *A Theology of Liberation*. Liberation theology is a wide field, though its most common formulation deals with political issues in Latin America.

Liberation theology says Christ came to liberate us not just from the spiritual effects of sin, but also from its temporal effects. In particular, it says Christians are called to help the poor change their social structures so they can be freed from the bondage of poverty. Liberation theology is also a "reflection on praxis," which is to say it learns from the practice of the Christian faith more than having the practice of the faith be derived from theological principles.

Now, on the surface, that all sounds fine. Jesus makes it clear that we have an obligation to care for the poor (Matt. 25:35–46) and the Bible repeatedly condemns rich people who exploit the poor. James 5 says, "Come now, you rich, weep and howl for the miseries that are coming upon you. . . . Behold, the wages of the laborers who mowed your fields, which you kept back by fraud, cry out; and the cries of the harvesters have reached the ears of the Lord of hosts" (vv. 1, 5). James 2 condemns showing favoritism to the rich, and the *Catechism* says, "Sins give rise to social situations and institutions that are contrary to the divine goodness" (1869).

Some aspects of liberation theology are correct, but there are other aspects that distort the gospel's message of salvation from sin through faith in Christ. These corrosive elements of liberation theology turn the eternal Faith into just another worldly social justice program—one that is often wedded to anti-Catholic ideologies.

Liberation Theology and Marxism

As I show in my book *Can a Catholic Be a Socialist?*, the Church has repeatedly condemned communism, socialism, and the other natural results of Marxist thought. But some defenders of liberation theology say Marxism isn't essential to it. Fr. David Inczauskis says,

> Accusations of Marxism have been at the center of magisterial critique, but most liberation theologians assert that they are not Marxists but that they make use of Marxism as a social science just as other theologians make use of non-Catholic philosophers like Aristotle in the case of St. Thomas Aquinas and Martin Heidegger in the case of Karl Rahner.[218]

St. Thomas Aquinas's use of the truths found in Aristotle is not the same as the errors of Marxism, which are at the forefront of liberation theology. Gutierrez says liberation theology seeks a more radical change than traditional "development," so it requires "a radical break from the status quo, that is, a profound transformation of the private property system."[219] He then talks about how in Latin America, Christians and Marxists seek more than a "theoretical dialogue" and then references the communist dictator Fidel Castro's praise of liberation priest Camillo

Torres as a symbol of "revolutionary unity."[220] I'm sure Castro made good use of Torres's repeated assertion that "if Jesus were alive today, he would be a *guerrillero*."

In *The Communist Manifesto*, Karl Marx said, "The theory of the communists may be summed up in the single sentence: abolition of private property."[221] Liberation theologian José Miranda goes even further, claiming that Marxism's primary errors are its atheism and materialism, rather than its view of human beings and their natural rights. As a result, he says that not only is communism not an error, but for a Christian to be anti-communist is, in his words, "the greatest scandal of our century."[222]

Compare this to papal encyclicals like *Quadragesimo Anno* (In the Fortieth Year) and *Rerum Novarum* (Of New Things), where the popes affirm a natural right to private property and that capitalism itself is not evil. Pope Leo XIII said socialism is contrary to the natural right to own property and that "the main tenet of socialism, [the] community of goods, must be utterly rejected" (*Rerum Novarum* 15). Pope Pius XI bluntly condemned any notion of Christian communism when he said, "Communism is intrinsically wrong, and no one who would save Christian civilization may collaborate with it in any undertaking whatsoever" (*Divini Redemptoris* 58).

The Poor vs. the Church

One example of how eternal life is squeezed out of the Faith through liberation theology can be found in Fr. Jon Sobrino's attempt to "rethink" martyrdom.

Traditionally, a martyr is someone who chooses death instead of renouncing the Christian faith. The Magisterium has developed this definition, like when it declared Fr. Maximilian Kolbe a martyr of charity because he died in the place of another man in a concentration camp. However, Sobrino goes way beyond any sensible development by claiming that martyrdom can be applied to *anyone* who dies because he was trying to enact structural change on behalf of the poor. He writes,

> In our time, "martyrdom" has, then, taken on a new form. Many men and women have suffered violent deaths not on account of their witness to faith but because of the compassion that stems from their faith. In the Church, these have been bishops and sisters, catechists and delegates of the word; in civil society, they have ranged from peasants and indigenous inhabitants to students, lawyers, and journalists.[223]

Sobrino says martyrdom can even be applied to *non-Christians* who die while fighting for the poor. Sobrino calls these people "Jesus martyrs" and says,

> Jesus martyrs are not, strictly speaking, those who die for Christ, but those who die like Jesus and for the cause of Jesus. Their martyrdom does not result from fidelity to some mandate of Jesus', or even from a desire for mystical identification with the crucified Jesus, but arises out of their effective following of Jesus.

Some liberation theologians treat the poor almost as if they have a special salvific status solely by virtue of their poverty and lack sins needing atonement that are found among the upper classes. According to Leonardo Boff, "from the moment when God became man-poor, man-poor became the measure of all things."[224] Gutierrez likewise says, "Since the Incarnation, humanity, every human being, history, is the living temple of God. The 'profane,' that which is located outside the temple, no longer exists."[225] And Sobrino mysteriously opined, "The Spirit is present in the poor *ex opere operato*," and that the poor are the channel for finding the Church's mission.[226]

In its 2006 notification, the CDF applauded Sobrino's concern for the poor, but it noted that "the 'Church of the poor' assumes the fundamental position which properly belongs to the faith of the Church." The CDF said Sobrino "reduces redemption to moralism" and reduces salvation to mere imitation of Christ instead of sacramental reception of Christ.[227] It also criticized Leonardo Boff and prohibited him from teaching theology because his book *Church: Charism and Power* privileges the poor above all others, including the Church:

> [In his own words, Boff claims that] "Jesus did not have in mind the Church as institution but rather that it evolved after the Resurrection, particularly as part of the process of de-eschatologization" (p. 74). Consequently, for him the hierarchy is "a result" of "the powerful need to organize" and the "assuming of societal characteristics" in "the Roman and feudal style" (p. 40). Hence the necessity arises for permanent "change in the Church" (p. 64); today a "new Church" must arise (p. 62 and *passim*), which will be "an alternative for the incarnation of new ecclesial institutions whose power will be pure service" (p. 63).[228]

In other words, Boff says we don't need a Church because the people, especially the poor, are the Church. But the poor aren't our saviors. The poor need to be saved because *every* human being needs to be saved from sin.

That doesn't mean the Church ministers to every human being in the same way. The *Catechism* says,

Those who are oppressed by poverty are the object of a preferential love on the part of the Church, which, since her origin and in spite of the failings of many of her members, has not ceased to work for their relief, defense, and liberation through numerous works of charity, which remain indispensable always and everywhere (2448).

Notice that although the Church rejects major components of popular liberation theologies, it does not reject the need to liberate the poor and show them a special kind of love. But that is because of the unique hardships the poor endure, not because they do not need eternal life.

Rich people and poor people can be enslaved to sin. Some sins are universal, whereas others are more or less common among certain classes (e.g., the extreme poor are rarely gluttons). But for many liberation theologians, salvation isn't about Christ saving humanity—it is about siding with the oppressed against the oppressor class.

Seeking True Liberation

Honest people open to God's spirit know they must be saved from their sinful rejection of God, and not just from evils of this life. For Catholics who seek a remedy that liberation theologians don't offer, many have left the Church for Protestant denominations that put Christ firmly in the center of their soteriology. The *Wall Street Journal* painted a bleak picture of the Church's decline in a 2022 article entitled "The Catholic Church Is Losing Latin America":

For centuries, to be Latin American was to be Catholic; the religion faced virtually no competition. Today, Catholicism has lost adherents to other faiths in the region, especially Pentecostalism, and more recently to the ranks of the unchurched. . . . The rise of liberation theology in the 1960s and '70s, a time when the Catholic Church in Latin America increasingly stressed its mission as one of social justice, in some cases drawing on Marxist ideas, failed to counter the appeal of Protestant faiths. Or, in the words of a now-legendary quip, variously attributed to Catholic and Protestant sources: "The Catholic Church opted for the poor and the poor opted for the Pentecostals."[229]

Ironically, liberation theologians seem to be aware of this problem, though they blame the poor for clinging to religious piety instead of joining their social revolution. One scholar of liberation theology notes that,

> despite claims to speak for the people (to be the "voice for the voiceless"), liberationist discourse has often remained alien to its intended clients. Being a voice for the voiceless is not the same as letting the voiceless speak, and even with the best intentions, liberationist activists have had problems shedding directive and paternalistic roles.[230]

The CDF's 1986 response to liberation theology gets it right when it says we must listen to the poor to discover what they truly need and not impose our political agendas upon them. It says,

> It is the poor, the object of God's special love, who understand best and as it were instinctively that the most radical liberation, which is liberation from sin and death, is the liberation accomplished by the death and resurrection of Christ. . . . It would be criminal to take the energies of popular piety and misdirect them toward a

purely earthly plan of liberation, which would very soon
be revealed as nothing more than an illusion and a cause
of new forms of slavery. Those who in this way surrender
to the ideologies of the world and to the alleged necessity
of violence are no longer being faithful to hope, to hope's
boldness and courage, as they are extolled in the hymn to
the God of mercy that the Virgin teaches us.[231]

Now, some people might say there's nothing wrong with
liberation theology since Pope Francis embraces it. Except
Pope Francis is not a traditional "liberation theologian."
He has joked about his critics calling him a "communist"
and has called for greater dialogue between Christians and
Marxists. But even liberation theologians are hesitant to
claim Pope Francis as one of their own.

Leonardo Boff certainly doesn't do that. Instead, he says,
"The important thing is not to be for liberation theology but
for the liberation of the oppressed, the poor, and the victims
of injustice, and that [Pope Francis] is without question."[232]
Dean Dettloff, an author of articles like "The Catholic Case
for Communism," writes in his 2021 article "Is Pope Francis
a Liberation Theologian?" that

Francis was not part of the rising tide of liberation theology. As someone born in 1936 who was part of a religious
order that became known for social justice, this was not
for lack of opportunity. His social conscience is informed
more by the "Theology of the People," a movement that
paralleled liberation theology and prioritized the poor,
but one that is unique to Argentina, drawing less on soci-
ological analysis and Marxist literature. . . . Francis could
have been a liberation theologian. He chose not to be.[233]

In closing, let me say that when Jesus spoke in the synagogue, he said that the words of Isaiah—promising a deliverer who would "proclaim good news to the poor," "release the captives," "set at liberty those who are oppressed," and "proclaim the acceptable year of the Lord"—had been fulfilled in their presence (Luke 4:18). The year he was talking about was the jubilee, which was celebrated every fifty years in Israel and involved the cancellation of debts, the freeing of slaves, and most importantly the remission of sins that were seen as the ultimate debt we could never pay.

In the year 2000, the Catholic Church declared its own jubilee and celebrated genuine liberation through Christ, saying, "Jesus comes to offer us a salvation which, although primarily a liberation from sin, also involves the totality of our being with its deepest needs and aspirations. Christ frees us from this burden and threat and opens the way to the complete fulfillment of our destiny."[234]

16

DEPORTATION

Immigration is a complex issue, and the Church wisely rejects two false approaches to it. On the one hand, the Church affirms that people have a right to migrate, and so countries should not absolutely prohibit immigration. Absolute prohibitions can lead to a callous disregard for human life, such as in 1939, when the Cuban, U.S., Canadian, and British governments all refused safe passage for a ship carrying over 900 Jewish refugees from Nazi Germany. The ship eventually returned to mainland Europe, where it is estimated that a quarter of its passengers were killed in the Holocaust.[235]

On the other hand, the Church rejects the view that governments must allow anyone to enter and remain within their nations' borders for any reason. The right to immigrate can be legally restricted, or as the *Catechism* says, "Political authorities, for the sake of the common good for which they are responsible, may make the exercise of the right to immigrate subject to various juridical conditions" (2241). These conditions entail that some people will not be permitted to immigrate into a country and, if they illegally do so, they will face legal punishments, including deportation.

However, some Catholics claim that the Church teaches that deportation is evil or even that it is *intrinsically* evil, meaning never permissible under any circumstance. Rachel Amiri of Where Peter Is writes, "It is worth recalling that deportation is evil, and that Catholics affirm that all human beings possess a God-given right to migrate. . . . St. John Paul II affirmed that deportation is an 'intrinsically evil act,' one that cannot be morally justified due to the way in which it offends against human dignity."[236] Amiri also cites an article in a journal affiliated with the Catholic Health Association of the United State that claims, "The Catholic moral tradition has identified deportation—not simply mass deportation—with strong, morally objectionable language."[237]

Defining "Deportation"

Those who claim that deportation is intrinsically evil, or always wrong, often cite *Veritatis Splendor* (The Splendor of Truth) and *Gaudium et Spes* (Joy and Hope). In the former document, Pope John Paul II discusses the issue of intrinsic evils, saying, "Reason attests that there are objects of the human act which are by their nature 'incapable of being ordered' to God, because they radically contradict the good of the person made in his image. These are the acts which, in the Church's moral tradition, have been termed 'intrinsically evil'" (80). The pope then cites the Second Vatican Council document *Gaudium et Spes* to provide specific examples of intrinsic evils, among which he lists "subhuman living conditions, arbitrary imprisonment, deportation, slavery, prostitution, and trafficking in women and children."

Those who argue that deportation is evil (generally or intrinsically) usually cite this passage, but it's important to clarify what is meant by the word *deportation*.

The U.S. government defines *deportation* as "the formal removal of a foreign national from the U.S. for violating an immigration law."[238] Most other countries would probably define the word in a similar way, so right away we should be suspicious that deportation is as evil as sex-trafficking, slavery, or prostitution. The evils in this part of *Gaudium et Spes* all relate to treating human beings like disposable property, but proportionately punishing someone for breaking a law does not treat him like property—it treats him like a person who is morally accountable for his actions.

The Latin word *deportatio* used in *Gaudium et Spes* has the same basic range of meaning as the English word "deport."[239] Every mention of the word "deport" prior to *Gaudium et Spes* uses the word as a synonym for *comportment*, or as a way of conducting oneself. However, immigration was an important issue during this time period, but magisterial texts do not treat it as being evil. The Vatican deported criminals who sought refuge in the Holy See, and in an address to members of the U.S. Senate, Pope Pius XII mentioned immigration from Europe due to the aftermath of the Second World War. He said,

> The question of immigration today . . . presents wholly new problems. As always the welfare of the country must be considered as well as the interest of the individual seeking to enter, and in the nature of things circumstances will at times dictate a law of restriction. But by the same token circumstances at times will almost cry out for an easing of the application of that law. Wise legislation will ever be conscious of humanity and the calamities, distress, and woes to which it is heir.[240]

The pope was probably referring to instances like the one we discussed earlier, of countries refusing entry to Jewish refugees from Germany who were murdered upon being returned to their homeland. But notice that Pius does not condemn deportation itself. He even acknowledges that restrictions on immigration will need to be made but that governments should in grave circumstances mercifully consider exceptions to those restrictions.

"Deportation" After Vatican II

After *Gaudium et Spes*, the word "deport" occurs in various documents on the Vatican website. In about two dozen cases, it refers to ancient Jews sent into Babylon or St. John's exile on the island of Patmos. Most often, or in nearly fifty cases, the word refers to mass deportations that are part of an organized campaign to commit genocide and ethnic cleansing. Pope Francis's address on the seventieth anniversary of the 1943 deportation of Jews from Rome to concentration camps like Auschwitz is one such example. Another is a 1978 address from Pope John Paul II, who said, "Courageous men must be sought not only on battlefields, but also in hospital wards or on a bed of pain. Such men could often be found in concentration camps or in places of deportation. They were real heroes."[241]

"Deport" is also used to describe totalitarian regimes like the Soviet Union that expelled dissenters into wilderness areas unfit for human habitation. In 2001, John Paul noted this transition from fascist persecution to communist persecution, saying, "Liberation from Nazism marked the return of a regime which continued to trample on the most elementary human rights, deporting defenseless citizens, imprisoning dissidents, persecuting believers, and even attempting to erase the very idea of freedom."[242]

After Francis visited the former Soviet state of Estonia in 2018, he said, "I went to the monument to the memory of those who were condemned, killed, tortured, deported. That day—I'll tell you the truth—I was destroyed."[243] The Church's *Compendium on Social Doctrine* mentions deportation only once, and it also links it to genocide:

> The solemn proclamation of human rights is contradicted by a painful reality of violations, wars, and violence of every kind, in the first place, genocides and mass deportations, the spreading on a virtual worldwide dimension of ever new forms of slavery such as trafficking in human beings, child soldiers, the exploitation of workers, illegal drug trafficking, prostitution. "Even in countries with democratic forms of government, these rights are not always fully respected" (158).

The essay Amiri cites even notes this connection in the *Compendium* and expresses doubt concerning the moral status of deportation. It says,

> Theological scholarship must grapple with the Second Vatican Council's mentioning of deportation, John Paul II's identification of it as intrinsically evil, and subsequent references to mass deportation. Might the qualification of "mass" deportation be akin to moral distinctions between direct and indirect abortion? If so, is this distinction sufficient, or does moral wrongdoing linger in at least some instances of deportation per se?[244]

In the nearly 100 references to the English word "deport" on the Vatican website, I found only two instances where the word is mentioned in the context of expelling someone from a country because he has broken a law related to the immigration process. In both cases, the word is uttered by a reporter asking the pope a question.

Deportation and Pope Francis

In the first case, a reporter from *Reuters* told the pope that "Trump called the pope a political pawn. He also said that, if elected, he would build a wall 2,500 kilometers long between the United States and Mexico and deport 11 million illegal immigrants." The journalists asked what Pope Francis thought about such statements and whether a Catholic in the U.S. could vote for this kind of person. The pope replied, in part,

> A person who thinks only of building walls, wherever it may be, and not of building bridges, is not Christian. This is not in the gospel. What you were asking me, whom to vote for or not: I won't interfere. I only say: if a man says these things, he is not Christian. We have to see if he said these things, and thus I will give him the benefit of the doubt.[245]

In this exchange, it's not clear that the pope said Trump is "not Christian." Rather, a person who "thinks *only* of building walls" and not bridges, or "a man" who says "these things," meaning the things the reporter attributed to Trump, is not Christian. He may have intended to draw the journalists' attention to proper Christian behavior toward migrants. In any case, the pope doesn't say deportation is intrinsically evil, or even that it is evil in general.

More striking is a question the pope was asked during a flight from Colombia to Rome. In the context, the pope said it is important for young people to "find their roots" and their heritage. A reporter raised the issue of how "those young people can be deported from the United States." Pope Francis replied, "True enough, they lose a root. . . . It is a problem. But really I don't want to express an opinion on that case because I have not read about it, and I don't like to speak about something I haven't first studied."[246]

Notice that in response to a question about deportation, the pope doesn't immediately call it evil, but reserves his judgment about the matter. But the pope does not have similar hesitations when asked about intrinsic evils like abortion and euthanasia. Instead, he recognizes that there could be mitigating circumstances that justify deporting at least some people from the United States—which means that the pope does not think deportation is intrinsically evil, since no circumstance can justify an intrinsic evil.

In response, some liberal Catholics say that words like *expulsion* and *extradition* should be used to refer to moral means of removing someone from a country. They say this is like how *murder* refers to immorally ending a person's life, whereas *killing* can refer to morally ending a person's life. But whereas the Church has laid out what specific conditions make killing murder, it has done nothing comparable to define when moral extradition becomes immoral "deportation." Instead, it condemns immoral mass deportations unrelated to immigration policy and allows civil leaders to make prudential judgments about whether other deportations are just or unjust.

Catholics should continue to promote immigration policies that respect the right to migrate and treat migrants with compassion while also respecting the right of nations to maintain sovereign borders. However, defenders of the "deportation is intrinsically evil" view must rely on an overly literal reading of *Gaudium et Spes* and *Veritatis Splendor* and ignore the context provided by every other magisterial and papal witness on this issue. Although the Magisterium could, in the future, place greater moral restrictions on modern deportation practices given changes in various social structures, for now, it has not taught anything remotely near the claim that deportation is intrinsically or even generally, morally wrong.

17

GUN VIOLENCE

We saw in the previous chapters that, in the face of children being killed in the womb through abortion, some liberal Catholics wag their fingers at the thought of outlawing such procedures. They tell us that outlawing abortion doesn't reduce abortion; it only hurts innocent women, who might be trying to get medical treatment for miscarriages, and it fails to address the "root causes" of abortion, which is really a problem related more to poverty than to morality. And any lobbying from groups like the USCCB for pro-life laws is seen as an inappropriate intrusion of religion into politics.

But when a child tragically dies from gun violence in a school shooting, the script gets flipped.

In the face of this violence, we are told that addressing the root causes of gun violence isn't enough and legislative action must be taken. Catholics have a moral duty to pass "gun control laws," and the failure to support this kind of legislation involves disobedience to the bishops and a tacit endorsement of children being murdered. Any complaint about overly broad laws harming innocent gun owners is dismissed as a kind of idolatrous love for guns. For example, the *National Catholic Reporter* urges conservative Catholics to "value the lives and dignity of the people slaughtered more than they do the golden calf of artillery and ammunition."[247]

But when we examine the complex issue of gun violence, we see that although the Church clearly condemns this violence, it does not have a specific teaching about how society should prevent it.

Church Teaching on Gun Ownership

The *Catechism* says, "Someone who defends his life is not guilty of murder even if he is forced to deal his aggressor a lethal blow" (2264). It then quotes St. Thomas Aquinas, who said,

> If a man in self-defense uses more than necessary violence, it will be unlawful, whereas if he repels force with moderation, his defense will be lawful. . . . Nor is it necessary for salvation that a man omit the act of moderate self-defense to avoid killing the other man, since one is bound to take more care of one's own life than of another's.

The *Catechism* doesn't mention private gun ownership, nor does it specify what kind of weapons a person may possess that are capable of delivering a "lethal blow." Given the *Catechism*'s silence on the matter, it's reasonable to infer that there is nothing in principle that is wrong with private gun ownership. According to Jimmy Akin,

> I am not aware of any statements of the universal Magisterium dealing with the ownership of firearms by ordinary, responsible individuals. Neither am I aware of any papal statements on this subject, nor statements by bodies such as the Congregation [now Dicastery] for

the Doctrine of the Faith (CDF), which also exercises the universal Magisterium when its decrees are expressly approved by the pope (*Donum Veritatis* 18).[248]

Some liberal Catholics quote papal encyclicals as evidence that the Church opposes private gun ownership. These include Pope John Paul II's discussion of violence in *Evangelium Vitae*, where he talks about "the vast array of threats to human life." He gives as one example "the violence inherent not only in wars as such but in the scandalous arms trade, which spawns the many armed conflicts which stain our world with blood" (10). In an interview after the 2022 shooting at an elementary school in Uvalde, Texas, Pope Francis said, "It is time to say enough to the indiscriminate trafficking of arms."[249]

First, these condemnations are for immoral acts related to the selling of weapons, not responsible gun ownership. Everyone agrees that it is wrong to give or sell weapons to certain people. Just as bartenders shouldn't sell drinks to stumbling drunks, firearm dealers should not sell weapons to people who are clearly at risk of committing violent acts. That's why federal and state laws prevent felons and those with substance abuse issues from purchasing firearms. But none of this shows that it is wrong to manufacture and sell firearms.

A year before *Evangelium Vitae* was released, the Pontifical Council for Justice and Peace published a document on the international arms trade that said,

It is urgent to find an effective way to stop the flow of arms to terrorist and criminal groups. An indispensable measure would be for each state to impose a strict control on the sale of handguns and small arms. Limiting the purchase of such arms would certainly not infringe upon the rights of anyone.[250]

Once again, this implies that the problem is not gun ownership itself. The problem lies in circumstances where guns fall into the hands of dangerous individuals. But although the universal Magisterium denounces gun violence and urges prudence in the use of lethal force, it has not said what practical measures should be used to keep lethal weapons (including guns) out of the hands of those who would misuse them. In spite of this, Carol Glatz claims that the Church's position on guns "is resoundingly clear: firearms in the hands of civilians should be strictly limited and eventually completely eliminated."[251]

What is her evidence for this sweeping claim?

Aside from referencing unnamed "Vatican documents," Glatz says, "According to the *Catechism*, the right to use firearms to 'repel aggressors' or render them harmless is specifically sanctioned for 'those who legitimately hold authority' and have been given the duty of protecting the community."

Glatz is referring to where the *Catechism* discusses killing in self-defense and the responsibility of authorities to protect civil society. It says, "Those who legitimately hold authority also have the right to use arms to repel aggressors against the civil community entrusted to their responsibility" (2265). But this does not mean that the Church is denying members of the community the right to bear arms.

If that were Church teaching on guns, then we wouldn't expect the *Catechism* to say of firearms that "public authorities have the right and duty to regulate them" (2316), since this implies that civilians can own them under certain conditions. We also wouldn't expect the *Catechism* to give a set of conditions to justify armed rebellion against corrupt civil authorities (2243), since this implies that civilians would have access to firearms.

Glatz even admits that the only evidence for her claim is "almost hidden in a footnote" of a USCCB document on criminal justice published in the year 2000. It says, "We believe that in the long run and with few exceptions—i.e., police officers, military use—handguns should be eliminated from our society." The fact that this aspirational statement is hidden in a footnote shows that it is more of a hope of the bishops than a serious policy proposal. It certainly isn't a doctrinal teaching requiring assent from the faithful.

In *Donum Veritatis* (On the Ecclesial Vocation of the Theologian), the Congregation for the Doctrine of the Faith noted that "it could happen that some magisterial documents might not be free from all deficiencies. Bishops and their advisers have not always taken into immediate consideration every aspect or the entire complexity of a question" (24). This is especially the case when bishops make prudential judgments about how to resolve issues that lie beyond their area of expertise, such as gun violence.

So, although the bishops can lend their support to public policy proposals, including gun control legislation, that Catholics should respectfully consider, these proposals do not demand the same level of assent as when the bishops uniformly teach on a matter of faith and Christian life.

An Idolatry of Weapons?

Some Catholics portray those who oppose broad gun control policies as "idolaters" who love guns more than their neighbor or even God. Catholic professor Thomas Shannon decries "an idolatry of weapons," though his complaints ring hollow, given that he sees nothing immoral in the killing of the youngest unborn human beings.[252] Fr. Thomas Reese ups the rhetorical ante, saying, "America sacramentalizes guns. They are God's gift to the good and just to protect our way of life. This is heresy."[253]

Liberal Catholics also talk about an "epidemic of mass shootings" and bemoan the availability of "assault weapons" without considering the entire context of firearm ownership and use in America. For example, Michael Sean Winters says Congress should "bring back the assault weapons ban" and asserts that "assault weapons—the suspect in Colorado could fire thirty rounds without reloading—are the problem. Assault weapons and sin, and sin can't be effectively banned."[254]

But there is no agreed-upon definition of an "assault weapon," and many common hunting rifles are more powerful than alleged "assault weapons" like the AR-15.[255] The most common weapon used to commit gun violence, including suicides, homicides, and "mass shootings," is the handgun.[256] The 2006 Virginia Tech shooter killed thirty-two people with handguns and simply carried extra magazines for reloading.

Finally, mass shootings are extremely rare, and mass school shootings are even rarer. Since 1898, there have been approximately thirty "mass school shootings," or about one every four years. About eight children have died in mass school shootings each year since the Columbine shooting in 1999.[257] In contrast, most gun-related deaths, about 25,000 every year, are due to suicide.

This means Catholics can reasonably disagree about which public policies would be effective and feasible to combat the different types of gun violence. Some Catholics may want to support traditional "gun control" policies, but other Catholics may choose to support "gun violence control" policies instead that don't focus exclusively on limiting access to firearms. These could include

- increasing mental health services and public education campaigns to combat gun-related suicides;

- educating gun owners about proper storage of weapons and providing financial incentives, like rebates or tax credits, for owners to purchase safety items like gun safes; or

- passing "red flag" laws at the state level that allow law enforcement to confiscate weapons from individuals who clearly demonstrate that they are a danger to themselves or others.

What about gun homicides? Despite what people hear in the media, nearly all gun homicides are the result of gang violence and domestic abuse. Policies that could reduce this kind of gun violence include

- aggressively prosecuting individuals who illegally buy weapons for those who are ineligible to purchase them;

- funding police interventions to reduce gang violence. According to one study of homicide suspects by the University of Chicago Crime Lab, "around 90 percent had at least one prior arrest," and "approximately 50 percent had a prior arrest for a violent crime"[258]; or

- promoting open carry and concealed carry of weapons for self-defense.

Finally, what about mass shootings? Because these events are so rare, it is difficult to craft public policies to address them.

Most mass shootings covered in the media are committed with handguns by people who passed background checks, so many popular gun control measures aimed at preventing these incidents will not be effective.[259] Instead, a Catholic could propose policies like these:

- Encourage news organizations and social media outlets not to report or share stories about mass shootings. Research has shown that this coverage has a "contagious effect" and causes more mass shootings in the weeks following coverage of a previous tragedy.[260]

- Create security measures in schools and other targets of mass shootings in order to make them less vulnerable.

- Allow trained teachers to safely store firearms in their classrooms in order to prevent mass school shootings.

Idolatrous Self-Defense?

I want to be clear that I am saying Catholics *can* support the policies I've described, but they are not obligated to support them. Likewise, they *can* support more traditional gun control policies, but they aren't obligated to support those policies, either. Neither is obligatory because the Church does not have a teaching on the precise methods the state must undertake in order to prevent gun violence.

The Church also teaches that the State should prevent extreme poverty, crime, and war, but it allows civic officials to study, debate, and implement a variety of approaches to combatting these evils since the Church doesn't always know which approach will be the most effective in a given social context. The Church teaches that gun violence along with knife violence, bomb violence, abortion violence, and all other forms of violence against innocent persons must be illegal. But it does not teach that the State must ban guns that can be used for lawful purposes just as it does not teach that the State must ban abortion instruments like suction machines that can be used for lawful purposes like removing a deceased, miscarried child from a woman's body.

The claim that opposition to gun control involves a tacit endorsement of gun violence can also be leveled at liberal Catholics. For example, one way to prevent gun violence is to aggressively prosecute people who illegally buy guns for criminals. But liberal gun control advocates often oppose this policy because they claim that such prosecutions disproportionately affect non-white people, and so the polices are racist. Ironically, the first gun control laws in the United States were crafted with the explicitly racist purpose of preventing newly freed slaves from owning guns.[261]

Liberal Catholics also scoff at the idea of guns being used for self-defense. For example, religious studies professor Patrick McCormick says it is a kind of "idolatry" to believe that "possessing a handgun will supply me with the strength and security that my reliance on God might have supplied me with in the past."[262]

Does McCormick think it is idolatry to possess a fire extinguisher, an airbag, or any other device that can keep us safe from fatal threats? It would be idolatry to think a gun can do more than God can do. But it's just common sense to believe that God gave us brains that can make tools to help us survive, including weapons to use to defend ourselves against natural threats like wild animals and man-made threats like evil people.

A 2013 study from the Centers for Disease Control shows that guns are used in self-defense 500,000 to 3 million times a year in the United States.[263] A 2021 professional survey found that guns were used annually 1.7 million times for self-defense.[264] Even if we assume the lower figure and say the use of a gun prevented a fatality in only 10 percent of cases, that would still amount to guns *saving 50,000 lives every year*, or more than the number of people killed by guns. Keep in mind that whereas firearm deaths are always reported, many people don't report an incident where brandishing a weapon prevented an altercation that could have become fatal.

The effectiveness of different laws like concealed carry and open carry is an appropriate topic of debate, and Catholics can reach different conclusions about these and other policies. A Catholic can, in good conscience, reject these policies as being imprudent or ineffective ways to address gun violence. But by the same token, a Catholic can, in good conscience, reject policies like "assault weapon" and magazine bans as being imprudent or ineffective policies without, as some liberal Catholics say, idolatrously worshiping guns themselves.

18

CLIMATE CHANGE

Pope Francis's 2019 encyclical *Laudato Si* covers many different topics, but the one people connect most with the encyclical is climate change. However, Cardinal Gerhard Müller downplayed the encyclical's authority on these issues, saying, "Environmental policy is nothing [sic] to do with faith and morals." Joe Dantona at *Where Peter Is* said this was "one of the silliest and most dangerous positions I've ever seen a cardinal publicly express. . . . As a reminder to Cardinal Müller, encyclicals are still an authoritative form of magisterial teaching."[265]

Is Müller right that environmental policy does not belong to the realm of faith or morals? Or is Dantona right that we must respect authoritative teaching in papal encyclicals? The answer is that both are correct if each position is properly understood.

Our moral duty to care for the environment certainly falls under the umbrella of "faith and morals." The *Catechism* says we must have "a religious respect for the integrity of creation" (2415). However, just as the Church teaches that we must help the poor but allows diversity of thought on how to help them, the Church allows a similar diversity on how to show care for

God's creation. This means Catholics are not bound to accept a prudential judgment on climate change that liberal Catholics often promote: we must abandon fossil fuels and rapidly switch to solar and wind energy production.

For example, Doug Demeo says in *America* that Catholic institutions should divest from financial holdings in fossil fuel companies "in order to uphold their Catholic mission."[266] Fr. Joshtrom Kureethadam, who heads up the Vatican's "ecology and creation sector," called the rejection of fossil fuels a moral and theological "imperative."[267] The editorial staff of the *National Catholic Reporter* lamented in 2023 that no U.S. diocese had divested from fossil fuels and criticized the U.S. bishops for not taking a "(relatively easy) step toward a more just future—or any future, for that matter—for life on earth."[268]

And then there's Fr. Thomas Reese, who wishes the pope would declare "climate change deniers heretics and put their books, articles, Facebook pages, and tweets on the Index of Forbidden Books." He also confesses that "nothing would give me more illicit pleasure than having the governors of Florida and Texas, along with the leaders of the oil and coal industries, excommunicated."[269]

But whereas Catholics are obligated to care for the environment and promote human welfare through sound policies, they are free to debate the benefits and downsides of using fossil fuels.

The Church and Climate Change

In 2021, a group of professors and students from Creighton University (a private Catholic school) reviewed about 12,000 columns published by U.S. bishops between 2014 and 2019 and found that 0.8 percent mentioned climate change, and those citations came from 26 percent of U.S. bishops. The authors complain that 47 percent of these columns "did not describe [climate change] as a religious issue about which the Catholic Church has established teaching."

But even among those that do treat climate change as a "religious issue," the authors are concerned that 59 percent of the columns studied "did not clearly convey the bishop's personal view about the teaching. Since silence can be a form of climate change denial, readers could interpret their bishop's silence of opinion as disagreement with Church climate change teaching and license for their own dissent."[270]

Dissent? Established teaching? The authors of the study (who are experts in sociology rather than theology) overstate the authority of the Church's teaching on climate change. Any *authoritative* teaching on climate change would relate to the following claims:

1. Climate change exists.

2. Climate change has an overall negative effect on human flourishing.

3. Humans have the ability to prevent or reverse climate change.

4. Humans have a duty to prevent a rise in global temperatures.

5. The duty to prevent climate change includes the duty to transition away from fossil fuels.

Claims 1-3 are empirical claims about the nature of the world that do not involve doctrines of the Faith or even moral judgments. They may very well be true, but just as the Church did not have the authority to affirm the scientific truth of heliocentrism in the Middle Ages, the Church does not have the authority to affirm scientific truths related to the warming of earth and its relation to human activity. *Laudato Si* even says, "The Church does not presume to settle scientific questions or to replace politics" (188).

This is good because science is a tentative enterprise and future discoveries can change or even overturn previous scientific conclusions. Galileo, for example, was correct about the planets orbiting the sun, but he was wrong about them doing so in a perfect circle. This doesn't mean science is completely unreliable; it just means that the Church's ability to teach the faithful is restricted to what God has revealed to the Church and anything that directly follows from that revelation, or the area of "faith and morals." As Cardinal Caesar Baronius said during the Galileo controversy, "the Bible teaches us how to go to heaven, not how the heavens go."

So, when Dantona "reminds" Cardinal Müller that "encyclicals are still an authoritative form of magisterial teaching," he is correct—but only in the parts of the encyclical that assert magisterial teaching.

As Catholic apologist Jimmy Akin shows in his book *Teaching with Authority*, papal encyclicals contain statements of doctrine as well as non-doctrinal statements like summaries of scientific opinions.[271] In *Laudato Si*, this can be seen in statements like "The problem [of warming temperatures] is aggravated by a model of development based on the intensive use of fossil fuels, which is at the heart of the worldwide energy system" (23). Since those statements are not Church teachings (i.e., doctrine), Catholics are not required to give religious assent to them.

What about claims 4-5? Does the Church teach that we have a moral duty to prevent climate change, including through the reduction of fossil fuels?

Along with non-doctrinal statements of fact, magisterial documents also contain non-doctrinal statements of "aspiration" that exhort actions but do not formally command the faithful. For example, consider when Pope Pius XI said in *Quadragesimo Anno*, "Mothers, concentrating on household duties, should work primarily in the home or in its immediate vicinity" (71). This didn't mean women had (or continue to have) a moral obligation only to care for the home and may not work outside it.

Pius's exhortation was written in the context of women working outside the home to the neglect of their families to supplement a husband's low wages (which he called "an intolerable abuse"). It is an aspirational exhortation for society to create better working conditions, not a teaching keeping all mothers at home that requires the religious submission of mind and will. Likewise, *Laudato Si*'s exhortations about the "urgent need" for fossil fuels to be "replaced without delay" (165), or the pope's 2023 apostolic exhortation *Laudate Deum* (Praise God)'s goal of the "abandonment of fossil fuels" (55), does not morally mandate Catholics to reject fossil fuels.

But why would encyclicals or other magisterial documents contain non-magisterial declarations?

Bishops, including the pope, don't simply propound what the Church teaches. They often seek to apply those teachings in different historical, social, and cultural contexts and in the face of novel challenges. As a result, the bishops may want to urge Catholics (and even non-Catholics) to promote the common good and defend the dignity of every person without *imposing* a particular teaching for them to accept on that matter. They may instead be *proposing* a particular set of approaches to these novel circumstances, especially if they are addressing non-Catholics. In fact, *Laudato Si* and *Laudate Deum* are addressed to "people of good will," which means that only a minority of the intended audience is Catholic. Given this wide audience, *Laudato Si* says it offers "broader proposals for dialogue and action" (15) and admits that "on many concrete questions, the Church has no reason to offer a definitive opinion; she knows that honest debate must be encouraged among experts, while respecting divergent views" (61).

Catholics should seriously consider non-magisterial papal proposals to improve things like familial and ecological stability, even if these proposals are not doctrines that require religious assent. As a result, Catholics may enthusiastically embrace them, or they may respectfully disagree with them. For example, a Catholic might say a pope hasn't taken into account other factors that mitigate the harms associated with mothers working outside the home or the use of fossil fuels, and so these things can be supported under certain circumstances.

Abortion or Climate Change?

Matthew Sitman says that if the bishops determine that abortion is pre-eminent because it attacks "life itself" and because "of the number of lives destroyed," then, he writes, "it's not clear why the climate crisis isn't just as urgent— a habitable planet is a precondition for 'life itself.'"[272] Fr. Thomas Reese says, "The climate apocalypse is real, and it is coming," and a contributor at *Where Peter Is* says we should give up things like "automobile-oriented transport system(s)" because that will at least support the "continued existence of a habitable earth!"[273]

But even scientific organizations and government research panels that stress the dangers of climate change admit that predicted rises in global temperatures won't destroy the planet or even the human race. At worst, we would experience a decline in efforts to reduce global poverty. For example, the worst-case scenarios (which experts now consider very unlikely) would result in a 13-percent loss in Global Gross Domestic Product by the year 2100.[274] The world would be poorer than it would have been, but even this wouldn't be as bad as the 25-percent loss of GDP that took place in just four years during the Great Depression (1929-1932).

What about the number of lives lost even if the human race survives? Fr. Reese says, "Many would argue that global warming is also a pro-life issue, as it puts millions of lives in future generations at risk."[275] Estimates of the number of future annual deaths due to climate change vary widely. The World Health Organization warns of 250,000 excess annual deaths, whereas a study in *Nature* puts it at 83 million deaths between 2020 and 2100 (about one million per year).[276] But 60 million born people die of all causes *every year*, and 73 million unborn children are aborted every year. Deaths related to climate change should be prevented, but the issue is not a "pre-eminent one" by any means.

Magisterial documents on climate change tend to focus on CO_2 emissions causing dangerous weather conditions and criticize those who deny this assumption (e.g., *Laudato Si* 23-26, *Laudate Deum* 5-19). But the documents don't address more nuanced views. One would be that although fossil fuel emissions can worsen some environmental harms to humans (and other species), fossil fuel use also lessens other environmental harms to humans (and gives us the ability to marshal resources so we can protect non-human species).

For example, life expectancy doubled in the century after the Industrial Revolution, when global temperatures increased one degree. That's because fossil fuels gave humanity the ability to reliably heat and cool buildings and widely distribute food and medicine in the face of unforgiving climate events like hurricanes and blizzards. Weather-related harms (the extent of which are also debated) due to increased CO_2 emissions have to be compared to the harm humans face when they lack reliable power and modern building materials (steel, insulation, etc.) made from fossil fuels. Even today, 90 percent of temperature-related deaths are due to extreme *cold* rather than extreme heat. One climate change columnist noted that "it is at least plausible that, as the paper's authors put it: 'The results indicate that global warming might slightly reduce net temperature-related deaths in the short term.'"[277]

Catholics can debate whether climate change initiatives designed to save lives are worth the lives they may inadvertently take through the lack of fossil fuels. But no similar comparison can be made to elective abortion. Unlike greenhouse gases, abortion is intrinsically evil, and, unlike fossil fuels, elective abortion doesn't save lives, nor does it promote the common good of society.

Finally, if a single country pledges to reduce CO_2 emissions, its efforts can be negated by countries that don't reduce CO_2 emissions. For example, *Laudate Deum* chides the United States for having twice the CO_2 emissions per person that China does (72) but neglects to mention that China produces twice as much CO_2 as the U.S. Moreover, whereas the U.S. has cut CO_2 emissions by 25 percent in the last twenty years, China has *tripled* its CO_2 emissions during the same time period.[278] But the individual lives saved from a country banning abortion can't be "negated" by other countries that don't protect the unborn. The life of every human being has intrinsic value, and each one represents a real increase of goodness in the world.

Even if U.S. policy could affect climate change at a global level, more lives could be saved with less costly methods. It would cost 23 trillion dollars to convert the U.S. power grid to one that relies solely on wind and solar energy (assuming that this is even possible).[279] Just 15 percent of that amount would end extreme global poverty.[280]

Moral Fossil Fuels

The economist Thomas Sowell once said, "There are no solutions; there are only tradeoffs." Every choice society makes will have its own benefits and drawbacks. That means that it is a fallacy to compare choices by looking at only the benefits of one choice and only the costs of another. The benefits and costs of all choices must be examined. For example, one contributor at *Where Peter Is* says, "The pope calls us to realize that our massive energy use is destroying both the natural world and the lives of the poor."[281]

But what is actually destroying the poor is their *lack* of access to clean electrical energy.

Access to clean electricity would help 2.6 billion people around the world who rely on cooking fuels like wood, coal, kerosene, and biomass (e.g. animal dung), which cause much more indoor air pollution than cooking with electricity or natural gas. The byproducts of burning these materials cause heart disease, lung cancer, and four million premature deaths—half of them in children under the age of five, who succumb to pneumonia after prolonged exposure to dirty air.[282]

In *Fratelli Tutti*, Pope Francis said that whereas "lack of access to electric energy was not considered a sign of poverty" (21) in the past, it is today, given the kind of flourishing humans can have in the modern world. The poorest people on earth will never escape poverty if they don't have reliable access to electricity. One research paper notes that "there are no high-income countries today with annual electricity consumption below 3,000 kWh per capita."[283] And it is not possible to give everyone on earth enough energy to have a decent life through renewable energy sources like solar energy, which would require tens of billions of solar panels along with unfeasible mega-batteries.

According to *Laudato Si*, "until greater progress is made in developing widely accessible sources of renewable energy, it is legitimate to choose the less harmful alternative or to find short-term solutions" (165). But what if the less harmful alternative will *always* be some form of fossil fuels because optimal renewable energy as a primary source of power may not exist for many generations (or even ever)? But the poor exist *right now*, and fossil fuels represent one of the least harmful ways to promote their well-being.

Is there a way to provide energy to the poor without relying on fossil fuels or impractical renewable energy? Yes—it's called nuclear power.

The Case for Nuclear Power

For many people, "nuclear power" conjures up images of radioactive time bombs. Part of this popular opinion was formed by fictional works like the 2018 HBO mini-series *Chernobyl* and the 1979 disaster film *The China Syndrome*.

But nuclear power is one of the safest forms of power in the world, easily beating out coal (which annually kills hundreds of thousands of people through pollution) and even solar energy (which annually kills dozens of people through falls from roofs during installation). Saying we shouldn't transition to nuclear power because of the Chernobyl disaster is like saying we shouldn't travel on ships because of the *Titanic*. Even the most recent nuclear disaster on record, the 2011 meltdown at Japan's Fukushima plant, resulted in only one death because of radiation (an employee diagnosed with cancer five years after the accident).[284]

In *Laudate Deum*, nuclear waste disposal is portrayed as a grim process that turns homes into graves "due to the diseases that were then unleashed" (30).* But advances in storage technology have also produced safe, reliable ways to store nuclear waste. Nuclear material can even be harvested from nuclear weapons, which would promote the Church's long-held aspirations of nuclear disarmament.[285] If 50 billion solar panels were used to power the entire world (seven panels for every person on earth), in thirty years, the panels would create a nightmarish amount of toxic waste due to the rare earth metals in the photovoltaic cells. In contrast, the entire world could be powered by just an additional 5,000 nuclear plants (or one plant for every 1.4 million people).[286]

Finally, nuclear power is much more reliable than wind and solar energy. Solar energy is at its weakest just before sunset. This is incredibly unfortunate, given that this is when consumer demand is at its *highest* due to people returning home from work at the hottest part of the day. Even places that have reliably gusty breezes can experience wind droughts, like the one that brought British turbines to a standstill in 2018 and caused a 40-percent reduction in energy production.[287]

---

* In response, the pope says, "It could be said that this is an extreme example, but in these cases there is no room for speaking of 'lesser' damages, for it is precisely the amassing of damages considered tolerable that has brought us to the situation in which we now find ourselves" (*Laudate Deum* 30). I confess that I do not understand what point the exhortation is making here, or even if it is referring to nuclear waste disposal. Suffice it to say, it does not provide a compelling reason to abandon the use of nuclear energy in order to reduce CO_2 emissions.

And yet, liberal Catholic approaches to climate change rarely mention nuclear power. *America* even ran a 2008 article arguing *against* nuclear power that is filled with all kinds of errors.[288] For example, it claimed that the need to mine uranium causes nuclear power to emit more CO_2 than solar or wind. But wind turbines and solar panels also cause pollution through the mining and manufacturing process. In a lifetime of energy production, a nuclear reactor emits the same CO_2 levels as wind turbines and one third the levels of solar panels.[289]

The article also claimed that "the government says that by the year 2050 atomic energy could supply, at best, 20 percent of U.S. electricity needs; yet by 2020, wind and solar panels could supply at least 32 percent of U.S. electricity." But in 2020, nuclear already reached the 20-percent production threshold, with wind and solar producing 12 percent of the nation's energy, not 32 percent.[290] This means we will probably never catch up with the French, who get 70 percent of their electricity from nuclear sources.[291]

In conclusion, the pope has used his public platform to endorse abandoning fossil fuels (such as in addresses at environmental events), but he has not bound the faithful to this judgment through the Church's Magisterium. At most, we can say the Church teaches that Catholics have a duty to care for the environment while remembering that the environment exists to serve human beings. In *Laudato Si*, Pope Francis even warns about undertaking efforts to protect the environment that negatively impact the poor (170-172).

To make an analogy, the Church teaches that we must show kindness to animals, but this does not preclude harming animals through meat consumption or pest control in order to promote human flourishing. Likewise, the Church teaches that we must respect the environment, but that respect doesn't preclude actions that change the environment for the benefit of human life. Consequently, a Catholic can legitimately ask if the benefits of producing greenhouse gases outweighs the harms associated with them.

CONCLUSION

In 1999, *Commonweal* magazine hosted a forum called "The Crisis of Liberal Catholicism." One of the contributors, Peter Steinfels, lamented the place of liberal Catholicism within the Church at the close of the twentieth century, which he termed a century of "irony" due to what he called collapsing "utopian dreams."

> Liberal Catholics have good reason to feel on the defensive and threatened from both within the Church and without. Rome considers us suspect, and has been pursuing a slow but steady policy of discrediting, marginalizing, and replacing us, and now and again, where the cost appears sustainable, rooting us out. The same goal is being similarly pursued by a number of influential, well-funded movements and publications that identify themselves as "orthodox" Catholics, presumably in distinction to the rest of us who are heretics. The most obvious and fundamental working difference between these groups and liberal Catholics turns on the possibility that the pope, despite the guidance of the Holy Spirit, might be subject to tragic error.[292]

How the tables have turned! During the pontificates of John Paul II and Benedict XVI, the most vociferous critics of the pope were those who flirted with endorsements of contraception or women's ordination. But now that over a decade has passed in the pontificate of Pope Francis, liberal Catholics are no longer on the defensive. Indeed, the ones arguing that the pope has been subject to "tragic error" (or at least "imprudent blunders") are conservatives, who receive a rebuke from liberals, who claim they are just being faithful to the Holy Father.

Throughout this book, I have focused more on the actions of laypeople and priests, but there is no denying that Pope Francis, although he has taken positions on issues like transgenderism that have angered his liberal allies, has also sown a fair amount of confusion on key theological and moral issues. For example, as I was revising this manuscript in December of 2023, the Dicastery for the Doctrine of the Faith released *Fiducia Supplicans* (FS), a declaration allowing for blessings of *couples* (but allegedly not *unions*) who are in "irregular relationships"—including same-sex relationships. Although the document claims that this is a development from a previous 2021 decree from the DDF, at first glance, it seems to directly contradict that decree, which forbade blessing same-sex unions because the Church "cannot bless sin."

I won't give you a complete analysis of the document here—others have ably done that—but I will offer some thoughts on it and how FS reveals one of the greatest tragedies of liberal Catholicism.[293]

The document, in principle, is orthodox, because it speaks of sinners seeking "spontaneous" blessings in order to live better lives. The Church may not be able to bless the sins that unite a couple (which is why FS prohibits anything in the blessing that resembles a marriage rite, as some German Catholics were arguing for), but it can bless the *people* in the relationship in hope that they grow closer to God. Cardinal Víctor Manuel Fernández, the head of the DDF and author of FS, gave the example of a divorced and remarried couple asking a priest on a pilgrimage to bless them during a difficult period of unemployment and hardship to illustrate the spontaneous "ten- to fifteen-second" blessing he was imagining.[294] Pope Francis said in January of 2024, "One does not bless the union, but simply the people who together have requested it. Not the union, but the persons."[295]

However, something can be technically true but lead to scandal if it is uttered without qualification. For example, one reason the Marian title "Co-redemptrix" has fallen out of favor among recent popes is that without an immediate qualification, many Protestants think the term means that Mary equally redeemed us along with Jesus, which is blasphemous. The typical qualification is that the term means Mary "co"-operated with God to bring about our redemption by becoming the mother of our Redeemer.

Likewise, it is technically true that a priest can bless "gay couples," since every person can be blessed. For example, anyone in mortal sin can go up to receive a blessing during the reception of Communion at Mass. But the act of imparting this blessing is easily mistaken for a commendation of sin without the express qualification that the blessing is only for each individual to grow closer to God, not for the sinful union that binds them. (And this raises the thorny question of how one can bless a "couple" without in some way blessing the thing that makes them a couple.)

So, although the document can be read as orthodox in principle, one can object to its likely interpretation and effects in practice. Indeed, shortly after it was released, Fr. James Martin "spontaneously" blessed dissenting Catholic theologian Jason Steidl Jack and his so-called husband, in the presence of a photographer so that the blessing could be part of a story in *The New York Times*.[296]

Many have written about the backlash from bishops in Africa and Eastern Europe who have refused to implement FS. But the more interesting backlash I have seen is among liberal Catholics, who see FS as "too little, too late." One article in *The Nation* bears the headline, "Why LGBTQ Catholics Are Ambivalent About the 'Gift' of Same-Sex Blessings." It says in part,

> Less expected was the ambivalence, anger, and cynicism expressed by some LGBTQ Catholics. Mary Pezzulo, a bisexual woman in a heterosexual marriage who is well known as a Catholic blogger, complained that the declaration is "in some ways a laughably tiny concession. In other ways, it's a monumental step forward." Others have been less nuanced. When asked whether he and his husband would now have their relationship blessed by a priest, my best friend told me in language too colorful for *The Nation* what those priests could do to themselves.[297]

Throughout this book, we have seen that among liberal laypeople and even some priests, there is an enthusiastic push to overturn the theological apple cart and replace it with all kinds of heterodoxy. But the bishops, even the most liberal of them, have been slow to act with the same enthusiasm. Cardinal Jean-Claude Hollerich, who said in 2022 that the Church's teaching on homosexuality is "no longer correct," changed his tune a few months later:

> I fully believe in the tradition of the Church. And what is important in this process is not a change of doctrine. But what is important is to listen to everybody, to listen also to the suffering of people. I think of parents, for instance, of people concerned. And to have a change not of doctrine, but a change of attitude, that we are a church where everybody can feel at home. So I am not in favor of changing any doctrine.[298]

The people whom liberal Catholicism hurts the most are not the activist priests, theologians, laypeople, or vacillating bishops. It's the average person whose love for the Church makes his commitment to remain Catholic inconceivable to his liberal friends, who say, "You know the Church is wrong on LGBT issues. Why not join a church that fully affirms LGBT instead of giving these paltry breadcrumbs like ten-second blessings?"

These average Catholics remain, and even they aren't entirely sure why. Part of it may be that they are like Charlie Brown, who sees the liberal football of "doctrine changing" and thinks maybe this time Lucy won't snatch it away. They listen to Fr. Martin and other prominent liberal Catholics and think, "Soon, soon the Church will apologize and change and treat us right." And Fr. Martin stokes this nonsense when he is portrayed in documentaries like *Building a Bridge* (2021) on a rooftop garden in New York, musing about how the seeds he plants need time, but one day, they will sprout, and spring will come for them. (They really beat you over the head with the symbolism.)

Later in the film, Fr. Martin visits a family with transgender children, and one of them says, "Hearing Fr. James Martin talk about that—we're at the beginning of what could be a great change to the Church—is helping me, I think."[299] Another young man makes the point more bluntly that he doesn't see how one can reconcile Fr. Martin's optimistic message about self-identified LGBT people "leading the Church" with the Church's official teaching on homosexuality: "I don't think I can find a place where both of them fit as much as my father has tried. As much as [Fr. Martin] has tried. There is a bit of doubt in my body, in my mind. I don't think—I don't think I'll find an answer to that question."

Deep down, these people know there are only two viable paths, neither of which involves the ambiguities present in the liberal Catholicism we've covered in this book.

You can cross the line Fr. Martin and other ambiguous liberal Catholics are unwilling to cross, and publicly express support for heretical feminist and New Age theology, legal abortion, and sodomy without subjective guilt because you're convinced the Church is wrong. Or you can be convinced by the Church, humbly accept its teachings (even if they are challenging), and strive to live in accord with them. What the *Catechism* says of Catholics who experience same-sex attractions is true for all of us who seek to be faithful Catholics: "By the virtues of self-mastery that teach them inner freedom, at times by the support of disinterested friendship, by prayer and sacramental grace, they can and should gradually and resolutely approach Christian perfection" (2359).

The liberal Catholicism I've critiqued in this book fails the people who need God and his Church the most. It causes them to downplay the spiritual hazard of certain sins (especially sexual sins) and retreat to a relativistic view of conscience and culpability. Because they haven't fully hardened their hearts by becoming full-blown dissenters, they can still hear God's voice calling them to repent of supporting or engaging in sins like sodomy and abortion. However, instead of responding to God's voice, they turn inward and find unhelpful outlets for their natural religiosity. For example, whereas they allow freedom of conscience for the most hardened sexual libertine who says he's Catholic, they fixate on Catholics who own guns or vote Republican, claiming they are really the ones who need to repent, because they are "ruining the Church."

I'll leave you with the words of Cardinal Francis George, in an address he gave in 1998, that are as true now as they were then, even if liberal Catholicism has received a "second life" during the pontificate of Pope Francis. It may be more popular, but the scandalous liberal Catholicism we've surveyed in this book still reaps the same empty harvest for souls:

We are at a turning point in the life of the Church in this country. Liberal Catholicism is an exhausted project. Essentially a critique, even a necessary critique at one point in our history, it is now parasitical on a substance that no longer exists. It has shown itself unable to pass on the Faith in its integrity and inadequate, therefore, in fostering the joyful self-surrender called for in Christian marriage, in consecrated life, in ordained priesthood. It no longer gives life.

The answer, however, is not to be found in a type of conservative Catholicism obsessed with particular practices and so sectarian in its outlook that it cannot serve as a sign of unity of all peoples in Christ. The answer is simply Catholicism, in all its fullness and depth, a faith able to distinguish itself from any cultures and yet able to engage and transform them all, a faith joyful in all the gifts Christ wants to give us and open to the whole world he died to save.

The Catholic faith shapes a church with a lot of room for differences in pastoral approach, for discussion and debate, for initiatives as various as the peoples whom God loves. But, more profoundly, the Faith shapes a church that knows her Lord and knows her own identity, a church able to distinguish between what fits into the tradition that unites her to Christ and what is a false start or a distorting thesis, a church united here and now because she is always one with the church throughout the ages and with the saints in heaven.[300]

ABOUT THE AUTHOR

After his conversion to the Catholic faith, Trent Horn earned three master's degrees in the fields of theology, philosophy, and bioethics. He serves as a staff apologist for Catholic Answers, where he specializes in teaching Catholics to graciously and persuasively engage those who disagree with them. Trent is the host of the *Counsel of Trent* podcast and has authored and co-authored more than a dozen books, including *The Case for Catholicism*, *Persuasive Pro-life*, and *Why We're Catholic: Our Reasons for Faith, Hope, and Love*.

ENDNOTES

1   Michael Sean Winters, "Liberal Catholics and the temptation of
    sectarianism" National Catholic Reporter (February 1, 2001). Available
    online at https://www.ncronline.org/opinion/distinctly-catholic/liberal-
    catholics-and-temptation-sectarianism.

2   Heidi Schlumpf, "Liberal Catholicism: We've been here all along" *National
    Catholic Reporter* (January 18, 2021). Available online at https://www.
    ncronline.org/opinion/ncr-connections/liberal-catholicism-weve-been-
    here-all-along.

3   "Openly Gay Catholic Priest Discusses Pope Francis' Appeal For LGBTQ
    Protections," National Public Radio (October 23, 2020). Available online
    at https://www.npr.org/2020/10/23/927015178/openly-gay-catholic-
    priest-discusses-pope-francis-appeal-for-lgbtq-protections.

4   https://twitter.com/JamesMartinSJ/status/1616870528794464257.

5   James Martin, "Like it or not, Pete Buttigieg is legally married" *Outreach*
    (January 23, 2023). Available online at https://outreach.faith/2023/01/
    like-it-or-not-pete-buttigieg-is-legally-married.

6   "Notification Regarding Sister Jeannine Gramick, SSND, And Father
    Robert Nugent, SDS★" Congregation for the Doctrine of the Faith (May
    31, 1999). Available online at https://www.vatican.va/roman_curia/
    congregations/cfaith/documents/rc_con_cfaith_doc_19990531_gramick-
    nugent-notification_en.html.

7   "USCCB President Clarifies Status of New Ways Ministry," USCCB
    (February 12, 2010). Available online at https://www.usccb.org/
    news/2010/usccb-president-clarifies-status-new-ways-ministry.

8   Joshua J. Mcelwee, "Pope Francis meets Jeannine Gramick, US sister
    known for LGBTQ ministry" *National Catholic Reporter*, (October 17, 2023).
    Available online at https://www.ncronline.org/vatican/vatican-news/pope-
    francis-meets-jeannine-gramick-us-sister-known-lgbtq-ministry.

9   *Building a Bridge* (2021). The relevant clip can be seen in my review of
    the film at "My review of Fr. James Martin's new documentary" (30:53).

Available online at https://www.youtube.com/watch?v=n9TrCqiyi_Q.

10   James Martin, "What is the official church teaching on homosexuality? Responding to a commonly asked question," *America* (April 6, 2018). Available online at https://www.americamagazine.org/faith/2018/04/06/what-official-church-teaching-homosexuality-responding-commonly-asked-question.

11   Robert P. George, "Fr. James Martin, Friendship and Dialogue, and the Truth about Human Sexuality," *Public Discourse* (June 17, 2018). Available online at https://www.thepublicdiscourse.com/2018/06/21846.

12   James Martin, "Six things we've learned during Outreach's first year," *Outreach* (May 1, 2023). Available online at https://outreach.faith/2023/05/six-things-weve-learned-during-outreachs-first-year.

13   Bill McCormick, "Bridging Truth and Love: An Interview with James Martin, SJ" *The Jesuit Post* (July 24, 2017) Available online at https://thejesuitpost.org/2017/07/bridging-truth-and-love-an-interview-with-james-martin-sj.

14   James Martin, *Building a Bridge: How the Catholic Church and the LGBT Community Can Enter into a Relationship of Respect, Compassion, and Sensitivity* (New York: HarperOne, 2018), 5.

15   Brandan Robertson, "The Bible does not condemn LGBTQ people," *Outreach* (October 9, 2022). Available online at https://outreach.faith/2022/10/brandan-robertson-the-bible-does-not-condemn-lgbtq-people.

16   Rabbi Danya Ruttenberg, "Rabbi Danya Ruttenberg: The "clobber verses" used against LGBTQ people are open to a diversity of interpretations" *Outreach* (July 2, 2023). Available online at https://outreach.faith/2023/07/rabbi-danya-ruttenberg-the-clobber-verses-used-against-lgbtq-people-are-open-to-a-diversity-of-interpretations.

17   "Whatever one may think of 'natural law' reasoning, it is not what Paul pursues. Rather, he works with an untested assumption that same-sex attraction and activity is not to be found among other animals." Harold W. Attridge, "New Testament passages on same-sex relations must be read in context," *Outreach* (October 2, 2022). Available online at https://outreach.faith/2022/10/harold-w-attridge-new-testament-passages-on-same-sex-relations-must-be-read-in-context.

18   "Anyone can see that straight persons also believe that they are the chosen of God. . . . And now, belatedly, we are able to see that the

reach of God's emancipatory love extends beyond straight people, who are readily approved by society, to include LGBTQ persons, who have been much too long held in the bondage of social censorship and social disapproval." Walter Brueggemann, "The Book of Amos shows how God's 'emancipatory embrace' includes LGBTQ people," *Outreach* (April 2, 2023). Available online at https://outreach.faith/2023/04/walter-brueggemann-the-book-of-amos-shows-how-gods-emancipatory-embrace-includes-lgbtq-people.

19   "Polyamory, therefore, is not equivalent to promiscuity. If individuals come together in committed relationship, I believe they are honoring the biblical paradigm for covenant, regardless of the number of people that may be involved." Brandan Robertson, *The Gospel of Inclusion: A Christian Case for LGBT+ Inclusion in the Church* (Eugene, OR: Wipf and Stock, 2019), 95.

20   Nicholas Shackel, "The Vacuity of Postmodernist Methodology," *Metaphilosophy*, vol. 36 (April 2005), 298-299.

21   "In the past few years, in fact, I've gotten several notes (perhaps four or five) from young men saying, in essence, 'I'm sorry I attacked you on social media a few years ago. I was young and dealing with my own sexuality. But I've just come out and am sorry.'" James Martin, "Like it or not, Pete Buttigieg is legally married."

22   Todd A. Salzman and Michael G. Lawler, "Conservative defense of Humanae Vitae is not just about contraception," *National Catholic Reporter* (February 6, 2023). Available online at https://www.ncronline.org/opinion/guest-voices/conservative-defense-humanae-vitae-not-just-about-contraception.

23   Kathleen Bonnette, "The first wedding my kids attend will be between two women. Here's what I hope they learn," *Outreach* (August 10, 2023). Available online at https://outreach.faith/2023/08/the-first-wedding-they-attend-will-be-between-two-women-heres-what-i-hope-my-kids-learn.

24   https://twitter.com/JamesMartinSJ/status/1187090285332967424.

25   https://twitter.com/JamesMartinSJ/status/1187409944104128516.

26   "The Outreach Guide to the Bible and Homosexuality." Available online at https://outreach.faith/bible/.

27   "Fr. James Martin: What does the Bible say about refugees, migrants and foreigners?" (February 13, 2017). Available online at https://www.youtube.com/watch?v=2BawKt1tAcI.

28 See for example "Dear Cathedral Family" (June 23, 2019). Available online at https://www.gocathedral.com/about/news-marketing/school-news/news-post/~board/homepagenews/post/dear-cathedral-family.

29 "Employees of Catholic Institutions Who Have Been Fired, Forced to Resign, Had Offers Rescinded, or Had Their Jobs Threatened Because of LGBT Issues" (September 21, 2021). Available online at https://www.newwaysministry.org/issues/employment/employment-disputes.

30 Luke Janiki, "We can (and should) do better by our Catholic L.G.B.T. school teachers," *America* (June 23, 2020). Available online at https://www.americamagazine.org/faith/2020/06/23/we-can-and-should-do-better-our-catholic-lgbt-school-teachers-238040.

31 James Martin, *Building a Bridge*, 49.

32 Hunter Stuart, "Holy Ghost Preparatory Teacher Allegedly Fired for Getting Gay Marriage License: Report," *The Huffington Post* (December 7, 2013). Available online at https://www.huffpost.com/entry/holy-ghost-teacher-fired_n_4405039.

33 Matt Malone, "The ministerial exception is good law—but no excuse for indiscriminate firing by Catholics," *America* (July 8, 2020). Available online at https://www.americamagazine.org/politics-society/2020/07/08/supreme-court-ministerial-exception-catholic-lgbt.

34 James Martin, *Building a Bridge*, 48.

35 "Address of John Paul II to the Bishops of the Provinces of Portland in Oregon, Seattle, and Anchorage on Their 'Ad Limina' Visit" (June 24, 2004). Available online at https://www.vatican.va/content/john-paul-ii/en/speeches/2004/june/documents/hf_jp-ii_spe_20040624_usa-bishops.html.

36 Mahita Gajanan, "Teacher Fired After School Discovers His Ties to White Nationalist Richard Spencer" *Time Magazine* (Jan 8, 2018). Available online at https://time.com/5093605/substitute-teacher-white-nationalist. Jonah McKeown, "Teacher fired for abortion rights social media posts sues Catholic school in SC," Catholic News Agency (July 11, 2019). Available online at https://www.catholicnewsagency.com/news/41769/teacher-fired-for-abortion-rights-social-media-posts-sues-catholic-school-in-sc.

37 James Martin, *Building a Bridge*, 48.

38 Paul Overberg and Anthony DeBarros, "Same-Sex Couples Accounted for 1 Percent of Households in 2020, Census Shows," *Wall Street Journal* (May 25, 2023). Available online at https://www.wsj.com/articles/same-sex-

couples-accounted-for-1-of-households-in-2020-census-shows-6bc23e58.

39 Marisa Lati, "School flying BLM, LGBTQ flags can't call itself Catholic, bishop says," *The Washington Post* (June 16, 2022). Available online at https://www.washingtonpost.com/religion/2022/06/16/school-blm-lgbtq-flags-not-catholic.

40 "Your thoughts on bishop request to remove BLM, gay pride flags," *National Catholic Reporter* (May 13, 2022). Available online at https://www.ncronline.org/news/opinion/ncr-today/your-thoughts-bishop-request-remove-blm-gay-pride-flags.

41 James Martin, "Can Catholics celebrate Pride Month? Yes, and here's why," *Outreach* (June 1, 2022). Available online at https://outreach.faith/2022/06/can-catholics-celebrate-pride-month-yes-and-heres-why.

42 "Tampa Bay Rays Players Decline to Wear Rainbow Logos for Pride Night. Pitcher Cites Jesus." *Yahoo! News* (June 6, 2022). Available online at https://www.yahoo.com/news/tampa-bay-rays-players-decline-102132583.html.

43 Cyd Zeigler, "Some Tampa Bay Rays players refused to wear a Pride rainbow, say they reject gay 'behavior,'" *Outsports* (June 5, 2022). Available online at https://www.outsports.com/2022/6/5/23155403/tampa-bay-rays-lgbtq-rainbow-pride.

44 Ryan Morik, "NHL analyst says Ivan Provorov can 'get involved' with Russia-Ukraine war after refusing gay pride jersey," Fox News (January 18, 2023). Available online at https://www.foxnews.com/sports/nhl-analyst-hradek-ivan-provorov-can-involved-russia-ukraine-war-refusing-gay-pride-jersey.

45 Elizabeth Payne, "Ottawa Catholic board to debate flying Pride flag," *Ottawa Citizen* (May 24, 2021). Available online at https://ottawacitizen.com/news/local-news/ottawa-catholic-board-to-debate-flying-pride-flag.

46 Jesse James Deconto, "Activist who took down Confederate flag drew on her faith and on new civil rights awakening," *National Catholic Reporter* (July 14, 2015). Available online at https://www.ncronline.org/news/justice/activist-who-took-down-confederate-flag-drew-her-faith-and-new-civil-rights-awakening.

47 Keith Lane, "Confederate flag removed from mural at Alabama school after protest" *WEAR News* (June 3, 2020) Available online at https://weartv.com/news/local/confederate-flag-removed-from-mural-at-alabama-school-after-protest-06-03-2020.

48 William Collins Donahue, "Schools in the North waved the Confederate flag, too. Now I know it wasn't innocent fun," *America* (July 7, 2020). Available online at https://www.americamagazine.org/politics-society/2020/07/07/michigan-school-spirit-and-waving-confederate-flag-was-it-ever-innocent-bit-fun.

49 Available online at https://www.usccb.org/resources/open-wide-our-hearts_0.pdf.

50 Eric Martin, "The Catholic Church Has a Visible White-Power Faction," *Sojourners* (August 2020). Available online at https://sojo.net/magazine/august-2020/catholic-church-has-visible-white-power-faction.

51 Mollie Wilson O'Reilly, "Suiting Up for Team Racist," *Commonweal Magazine* (February 7, 2019). Available online at https://www.commonwealmagazine.org/suiting-team-racist.

52 James Martin, "Can Catholics celebrate Pride Month?"

53 "Pulse nightclub shooter intended to attack Disney, prosecutors say," CBS News (March 28, 2018). Available online at https://www.cbsnews.com/news/orlando-pulse-nightclub-shooter-omar-mateen-intended-to-attack-disney-shopping-complex-prosecutors-say.

54 Robert Shine, "Bishop: Pastors Must Deny Funerals to Catholics in Same-Gender Marriages," New Ways Ministry (June 22, 2017). Available online at https://www.newwaysministry.org/2017/06/22/bishop-pastors-must-deny-funerals-to-catholics-in-same-gender-marriages. See also Robert Shine, "Catholics Angered by Bishop's Attempt to Exclude Lesbian and Gay Couples," New Ways Ministry (June 24, 2017). Available online at https://www.newwaysministry.org/2017/06/24/catholics-angered-by-bishops-attempt-to-exclude-lesbian-and-gay-couples.

55 Richard Leonardi, "Never a Eulogy," *Catholic Exchange* (January 25, 2007). Available online at https://catholicexchange.com/never-a-eulogy.

56 Todd A. Salzman and Michael G. Lawler, "The scandal may be in not holding funerals for gay spouses, theologians say," *National Catholic Reporter* (January 16, 2018). Available online at https://www.ncronline.org/news/justice/funeral-rites-gay-spouses-public-scandal-eye-beholder.

57 Kathleen Bonnette, "The first wedding my kids attend will be between two women."

58 Alan Feuer, "Diocese of Brooklyn Denies Funeral Mass for Gotti," *The New York Times* (June 13, 2002). Available online at https://www.nytimes.

com/2002/06/13/nyregion/diocese-of-brooklyn-denies-funeral-mass-for-gotti.html.

59 Rosie Scammel, "Italian Catholic Church scrambles to explain role in lavish Mafia boss funeral," *National Catholic Reporter* (August 24, 2015). Available online at https://www.ncronline.org/news/world/italian-catholic-church-scrambles-explain-role-lavish-mafia-boss-funeral.

60 Patrick Reilly, "St. Patrick's Cathedral says it was tricked into hosting 'sacrilegious' transgender activist's wild funeral" *New York Post* (February 17, 2024). Available online at https://nypost.com/2024/02/17/us-news/st-patricks-cathedral-said-it-was-tricked-into-hosting-transgender-activists-funeral/.

61 Scammel.

62 Robert Shine, "Bishop: Pastors Must Deny Funerals."

63 John M. Huels, "Other Acts of Divine Worship," *New Commentary on the Code of Canon Law*, eds. John P. Beal, James A. Coriden, Thomas J. Green (New York: Paulist Press, 2000), 1,412.

64 "In the planning of funeral rites for those involved in such marriages, a distinction should be made between those who have tried to practice their faith to the fullest possible extent and those who have neglected it. In the first instance, Mass would usually be celebrated when requested by the family. In the second instance, the 'Funeral Liturgy Outside Mass' might be held in the church or at the funeral home." "Funeral Guidelines." Available online at https://www.bridgeportdiocese.org/wp-content/uploads/2015/10/Funeral_guideline_book.doc.

65 Brian Roewe, "Milwaukee Archdiocese takes aim at trans persons in sweeping new policy," *National Catholic Reporter* (January 26, 2022). Available online at https://www.ncronline.org/news/people/milwaukee-archdiocese-takes-aim-trans-persons-sweeping-new-policy.

66 "Catechesis and Policy on Questions Concerning Gender Theory." Available online at https://www.archmil.org/ArchMil/attachments/2022GenderTheoryfinal.pdf.

67 Synodal Forum IV: "Life in succeeding relationships—Living love in sexuality and partnership" for the Second Reading at the Fifth Synodal Assembly (March 9-11, 2023) for the implementation text "Dealing with gender diversity." Available online at https://www.synodalerweg.de/fileadmin/Synodalerweg/Dokumente_Reden_Beitraege/

englisch-SV-V/ENG_SV-V-Synodalforum-IV-Handlungstext.
UmgangMitGeschlechtlicherVielfalt_Les2.pdf.

68 J.D. Long-Garcia, "Vatican gender document makes one thing clear: The
church needs more dialogue," *America* (January 26, 2022). Available online
at https://www.americamagazine.org/faith/2019/06/14/vatican-gender-
document-makes-one-thing-clear-church-needs-more-dialogue.

69 Daniel P. Horan, "Recent transphobic statements from bishops make
truth claims without facts," *National Catholic Reporter* (September 1, 2021).
Available online at https://www.ncronline.org/news/opinion/faith-seeking-
understanding/recent-transphobic-statements-bishops-make-truth-claims.

70 Daniel P. Horan, "Why Catholics should use preferred gender pronouns
and names," *National Catholic Reporter* (October 13, 2021). Available online
at https://www.ncronline.org/news/opinion/why-catholics-should-use-
preferred-gender-pronouns-and-names.

71 Daniel P. Horan, "The truth about so-called 'gender ideology,'" *National
Catholic Reporter* (June 24, 2020). Available online at https://www.
ncronline.org/news/opinion/faith-seeking-understanding/truth-about-so-
called-gender-ideology.

72 Judith Butler, *Gender Trouble: Feminism and the Subversion of Identity* (New
York: Routledge, 1999), 117. I should note that Butler attributes this view
to the postmodern philosopher Michel Foucault, but she also agrees with it.

73 "Address of His Holiness Benedict XVI to the Members of the Roman
Curia for the Traditional Exchange of Christmas Greetings" (December
22, 2008). Available online at https://www.vatican.va/content/benedict-
xvi/en/speeches/2008/december/documents/hf_ben-xvi_spe_20081222_
curia-romana.html.

74 Daniel P. Horan, "Why I finally left Twitter (aka 'X')," *National Catholic
Reporter* (December 28, 2023). Available online at https://www.ncronline.
org/opinion/ncr-voices/why-i-finally-left-twitter-aka-x.

75 Mary Sullivan Beckley, "Liberal Catholic Priest Daniel Horan Rage-Quits
Twitter After People Pushed Back on His Pro-Transgender Post," *The
Daily Beast* (December 28, 2023). Available online at https://dailycaller.
com/2023/12/28/liberal-catholic-priest-dan-horan-quit-twitter-
transgender-notre-dame-college.

76 Daniel P. Horan, *Catholicity and Emerging Personhood: A Contemporary
Theological Anthropology* (Maryknoll, NY: Orbis Books, 2019), 161.

77   Courtney Mares, "Pope Francis: Gender ideology is 'one of the most dangerous ideological colonizations' today," Catholic News Agency (March 11, 2023). Available online at https://www.catholicnewsagency .com/news/253845/pope-francis-gender-ideology-is-one-of-the-most-dangerous-ideological-colonizations-today.

78   Peter Feuerherd, "New Pro-life Movement: 'No' to Trump; 'yes' to atheists," *National Catholic Reporter* (January 17, 2019). Available online at https:// www.ncronline.org/news/new-pro-life-movement-no-trump-yes-atheists.

79   William T. Cavanaugh, "Electing Republicans has not reversed Roe v. Wade. It's time to change our strategy," *America* (September 23, 2020). Available online at https://www.americamagazine.org/politics-society/2020/09/18/republicans-supreme-court-abortion-overturn-roe-v-wade-pro-life-catholic-trump.

80   Rebecca Bratten Weiss, "Overturning Roe would not be a pro-life win" *National Catholic Reporter* (May 16, 2022). Available online at https://www. ncronline.org/news/opinion/overturning-roe-would-not-be-pro-life-win.

81   "Maternal Mortality Ratio," The World Factbook, Central Intelligence Agency (2017). Available online at https://www.cia.gov/the-world-factbook/field/maternal- mortality-ratio/country-comparison. See also Donna Hoyert, "Maternal Mortality Rates in the United States, 2019," National Center for Health Statistics. Available online at https://www. cdc.gov/nchs/data/ hestat/maternal-mortality-2021/E-Stat-Maternal-Mortality-Rates-H.pdf.

82   Stephen P. Millies, *Good Intentions: A History of Catholic Voters' Road from Roe to Trump* (Collegeville, MN: Liturgical Press Academic, 2018), 103.

83   See "DIALOGUE: A Catholic Case for 'Roe v. Wade'?" (January 12, 2022). Available online: https://www.catholic.com/audio/cot/dialogue-a-catholic-case-for-roe-v-wade.

84   Steven P. Millies, "Will overturning Roe finally allow Catholics to pursue a consistent ethic of life?", Religion News Service (May 16, 2022). Available online at https://religionnews.com/2022/05/16/will-overturning-roe-finally-allow-catholics-to-pursue-a-consistent-ethic-of-life.

85   Emily Reimer-Barry, "Another Pro-life Movement Is Possible," *Proceedings of The Catholic Theological Society of America*, vol. 74 (2019), 21-41. Available online at https://ejournals.bc.edu/index.php/ctsa/article/view/11403.

86   *Id.*, 23.

87 Marjorie Hyer, "Curran Retains Teaching Job, Must Leave Theology School," *The Washington Post* (April 13, 1988). Available online at https://www.washingtonpost.com/archive/politics/1988/04/13/curran-retains-teaching-job-must-leave-theology-school/16804265-ba68-4603-b6b1-fb3c2182b23c.

88 Courtney Mares, "Pope Francis: 'I believe it is time to rethink the concept of a just war,'" Catholic News Agency (July 1, 2022). Available online at https://www.catholicnewsagency.com/news/251691/pope-francis-i-believe-it-is-time-to-rethink-the-concept-of-a-just-war.

89 This doesn't mean laws prohibiting abortion must always carry the maximum penalty for wrongdoing. They can also consider mitigating factors. For more, see Trent Horn, *Persuasive Pro-life: Second Edition* (El Cajon, CA: Catholic Answers Press, 2022), 197-202.

90 Emily Reimer-Barry, "Another Pro-life Movement Is Possible," *Proceedings of The Catholic Theological Society of America*, vol. 74 (2019), 35.

91 Michael Sean Winters, "On both sides of abortion debate, Catholics largely fall short," *National Catholic Reporter* (January 22, 2020). Available online at https://www.ncronline.org/opinion/distinctly-catholic/both-sides-abortion-debate-catholics-largely-fall-short.

92 Matthew Sitman, "Preeminent?", *Commonweal* (November 21, 2019). Available online at https://www.commonwealmagazine.org/preeminent.

93 Devin Watkins, "Pope to Pro-life Movement: 'Politicians should place defense of life first,'" *Vatican News* (February 2, 2019). Available online at http://www.vaticannews.cn/en/pope/news/2019-02/pope-francis-pro-life-movement-politicians-defend-life.print.html.

94 Tom Hoopes, "Bernardin: Put Life First," *National Catholic Register* (June 9, 2009). Available online at https://www.ncregister.com/blog/tom-hoopes/bernardin_put_life_first.

95 Todd A. Salzman and Michael G. Lawler, "The U.S. bishops should stop singling out abortion as the 'pre-eminent' issue for Catholic voters," *America* (June 7, 2021). Available online at https://www.americamagazine.org/faith/2021/06/07/us-bishops-2024-election-biden-abortion-catholic-voting-240785.

96 Robert W. McElroy, "Pope Francis makes addressing poverty essential," *America* (October 8, 2013). Available online at https://www.americamagazine.org/church-poor.

97 Charles C. Camosy and David McPherson, "Consistent-life-ethic
    Catholics can (and should) treat abortion as today's preeminent priority,"
    America (July 8, 2021). Available online at https://www.americamagazine.
    org/faith/2021/07/08/abortion-politics-us-bishops-eucharist-
    ethics-240991.

98 Rebecca Bratten Weiss, "Overturning Roe would not be a pro-life win."

99 Dench et al. "The Effects of the Dobbs Decision on Fertility," IZA DP No.
    16608 (November 2023). Available online at https://docs.iza.org/dp16608.pdf.

100 "Abortions in Texas fell 60 percent in the first month after its new law
    took effect," National Public Radio (February 10, 2022). Available online
    at https://www.npr.org/2022/02/10/1079963293/abortions-in-texas-fell-
    60-in-the-first-month-after-its-new-law-took-effect#:~:text=National-
    ,Abortions%20in%20Texas%20fell%2060%25%20in%20the%20first%20
    month,its%20new%20law%20took%20effect.

101 Michael J. New, "Analyzing the Effect of Anti-abortion U.S. State
    Legislation in the Post-Casey Era," *State Politics & Policy Quarterly*, vol.
    11, no. 1 (2011), 28-47. See also Katharina Buchholz, "Restrictive Laws
    Show Effect as U.S. Abortion Rate Declines," *Statista* (September 2, 2021).
    Available online at https://www.statista.com/chart/16950/abortion-rates-
    in-the-us-since-1984.

102 Aaron Blake, "States that are more opposed to abortion rights have fewer
    abortions—but not fewer unintended pregnancies," *The Washington Post*
    (January 29, 2015). Available online at https://www.washingtonpost.com/
    news/the-fix/wp/2015/01/29/states-that-are-more-opposed-to-abortion-
    have-fewer-abortions-but-not-fewer-unintended-pregnancies.

103 See "Vermont 2017 Vital Statistics 133rd Report Relating to the Registry
    and Return of Births, Deaths, Marriages, Divorces, and Dissolutions."
    Available online at https://www.healthvermont.gov/sites/default/files/
    documents/pdf/Vital%20Statistics%20Bulletin%202017.pdf. See also "State
    Facts About Abortion: Wyoming" at https://www.guttmacher.org/fact-
    sheet/state-facts-about-abortion-wyoming.

104 See "Abortion rate in Sweden from 2010 to 2020" at https://www.statista.
    com/statistics/565814/abortion-rate-in-sweden and Rachel K. Jones et al.,
    "Abortion Incidence and Service Availability in the United States, 2017,"
    Guttmacher Institute (September 2019). Available online at https://www.
    guttmacher.org/report/abortion-incidence-service-availability-us-2017.

105 Joanna Venator and Richard V. Reeves, "The implications of inequalities in contraception and abortion," Brookings (February 26, 2015). Available online at https://www.brookings.edu/blog/social-mobility-memos/2015/02/26/the-implications-of-inequalities-in-contraception-and-abortion.

106 Celia Wexler, "It Is Time to Revisit Church's Stance on Contraception," *Huffington Post* (September 7, 2017). Available online at https://www.huffpost.com/entry/it-is-time-to-revisit-chu_b_11879144.

107 "Humanae Vitae," *Catholics for Choice*. Available online at https://www.catholicsforchoice.org/resource-library/humanae-vitae.

108 Todd A. Salzman and Michael G. Lawler, "Conservative defense of Humanae Vitae."

109 Pope Pius XII, "Address to Midwives on the Nature of Their Profession" (1951). Available online at https://www.papalencyclicals.net/pius12/p12midwives.htm.

110 Paul Ehrlich, *The Population Bomb* (New York: Ballantine Books, 1968), 1.

111 "New documents reveal inner workings of papal birth control commission" (March 16, 2011). Available online at https://www.catholicnewsagency.com/news/new-documents-reveal-inner-workings-of-papal-birth-control-commission.

112 Robert McClory, *Turning Point: The Inside Story of the Papal Birth Control Commission and How Humanae Vitae Changed the Life of Patty Crowley and the Future of the Church* (New York: Crossroad, 1997), 48.

113 *Id.*, 105.

114 *Id.*, 122.

115 Robert Blair Kaiser, *The Encyclical That Never Was: The Story of the Pontifical Commission on Population, Family and Birth, 1964-66* (Sheed and Ward, 1987), 233.

116 *Id.*, 10.

117 Todd A. Salzman and Michael G. Lawler, "Conservative defense of Humanae Vitae."

118 Paul Gondreau, "Contraception Can't Be Reha-Pill-itated," Catholic Answers (March 7, 2023). Available online at https://www.catholic.com/magazine/online-edition/contraception-cant-be-reha-pill-itated.

119 Simon Caldwell, "Pope Francis upholds Catholic ban on contraception," *Catholic Herald* (May 2, 2023). Available online at https://catholicherald.

co.uk/pope-francis-upholds-catholic-ban-on-contraception.

120 Ralph McInerny, "Humanae Vitae and the Principle of Totality" in *Why Humanae Vitae Was Right*, ed. Janet Smith (San Francisco: Ignatius Press, 1993), 341.

121 Jonathan Liedl, "Back to the Sixties? Pontifical Academy for Life Pushes for Departure from Doctrine on Contraceptive Sex," *National Catholic Register* (July 13, 2022). Available online at https://www.ncregister.com/news/analysis-pontifical-academy-for-life-pushes-to-change-churchs-opposition-to-contraception.

122 "Archbishop Paglia on relevance of 'Humanae vitae' today," *Vatican News* (May 19, 2023). Available online at https://www.vaticannews.va/en/vatican-city/news/2023-05/archbishop-paglia-humanae-vitae-theology-sexuality-procreation.html.

123 "Vickey McBride Preaches for the Second Sunday of Lent" (February 28, 2021), 02:16. Available online at https://www.youtube.com/watch?v=UX-akEp58Dg.

124 James Martin, "God is not a man (or a woman)," *America* (March 8, 2021). Available online at https://www.americamagazine.org/faith/2021/03/08/is-god-a-man-or-a-woman-catholic-240173.

125 "Response to Observations by Sr. Elizabeth A. Johnson, C.S.J., Regarding the Committee on Doctrine's Statement About the Book *Quest for the Living God*" (October 11, 2011), p. 4. Available online at https://www.usccb.org/resources/response-to-observations.pdf.

126 Joseph Cardinal Ratzinger with Vittorio Messori, *The Ratzinger Report: An Exclusive Interview on the State of the Church*, trans. Salvator Attanasio and Graham Harrison (San Francisco: Ignatius Press, 1985), 97.

127 Joyce Rupp, "Who is Sophia in the Bible?", *U.S. Catholic* (January 4, 2016). Available online at https://uscatholic.org/articles/201601/desperately-seeking-sophia.

128 "The Acts of Thomas" in *The New Testament Apocrypha*, ed. M.R. James (Berkeley, CA: Apocryphile Press, 2004), 888.

129 Mary Daly, *Gyn/Ecology: The Metaethics of Radical Feminism* (Boston: Beacon Press, 1990), xiv.

130 *Id.*, 59.

131 Mary Daly, *Beyond God the Father: Toward a Philosophy of Women's Liberation* (Boston: Beacon Press, 1973), 31.

132 Mary Daly, *Gyn/Ecology*, 81.

133 Mary Daly, *Beyond God the Father*, 79.

134 "Mary Daly and the second sex," *U.S. Catholic*, vol. 34, no. 5 (September 1, 1968). Available online at https://uscatholic.org/articles/196809/45-years-ago-in-u-s-catholic-mary-daly-and-the-second-sex.

135 Mary Kate Holman, "Priesthood, Reimagined" *Commonweal* (May 5, 2021). Available online at https://www.commonwealmagazine.org/priesthood-reimagined.

136 Richard Rohr, *The Universal Christ: How a Forgotten Reality Can Change Everything We See, Hope For, and Believe* (New York: Convergent Books, 2019), 19.

137 Id., 172.

138 Letter to Cledonius, 5.

139 Richard Rohr, *The Universal Christ*, 19.

140 *Id.*, 32.

141 *Id.*, 17.

142 *Id.*, 177.

143 *Id.*, 134, 137

144 *Id.*, 6

145 Athanasius, *On the Incarnation* 1.

146 Richard Rohr, *The Universal Christ*, 19.

147 *Id.*, 12

148 "Jesus Christ the Bearer of the Water of Life: A Christian Reflection On The 'New Age,'" Pontifical Council for Culture, Pontifical Council for Interreligious Dialogue (February 3, 2003). Available online at https://www.vatican.va/roman_curia/pontifical_councils/interelg/documents/rc_pc_interelg_doc_20030203_new-age_en.html.

149 Richard Rohr, *The Universal Christ*, 196. In his book *What Do We Do with Evil?*, Rohr says of this passage that "these are almost certainly [Paul's] premodern words for what we would now call corporations, institutions, nation-states, and organizations." "The Spirits of the Air," The Center for Action and Contemplation (October 14, 2020). Available online at https://cac.org/daily-meditations/the-spirits-of-the-air-2020-10-14.

150 "The Inner Witness," The Center for Action and Contemplation (October 10, 2016). Available online at https://cac.org/daily-meditations/the-inner-witness-2016-10-10.

151 Richard Rohr, *The Universal Christ*, 236.

152 "The Passion (Richard Rohr)," John Mark Ministries (February 9, 2005). Available online at https://www.jmm.org.au/articles/14431.htm.

153 Richard Rohr, *The Universal Christ*, 182.

154 *Id.*, 196.

155 "Statement from Fr. Richard Rohr, O.F.M. after meeting Pope Francis," The Center for Action and Contemplation (July 1, 2022). Available online at https://cac.org/news/statement-from-fr-richard-rohr-ofm-after-meeting-pope-francis.

156 "What the Chosen Gets WRONG (part 2)," 03:03. Available online at https://www.youtube.com/watch?v=aqlO_fbMF5Q&t.

157 "They have at least as much in common with Graeco-Roman *Bioi*, as the *Bioi* have with each other. Therefore, the gospels must belong to the genre of Bios." Richard A. Burridge, *What Are the Gospels?: A Comparison with Graeco-Roman Biography* (Grand Rapids: Wm. B. Eerdmans, 2004), 250.

158 Eusebius, *Church History* 3:39.

159 I. Howard Marshall, *Luke: Historian and Theologian*, third edition (Downer's Grove, IL: InterVarsity Press, 1998), 18.

160 Thucydides, *History of the Peloponnesian War*, 1.22.1.

161 "What the Chosen Gets WRONG (part 2)," 04:57. Available online at https://www.youtube.com/watch?v=aqlO_fbMF5Q&t.

162 https://twitter.com/caseyofm/status/1443395467371597835.

163 Paweł Rytel-Andrianik, "100 years of the Studium Biblicum Franciscanum in Jerusalem," *Vatican News* (January 17, 2024). Available online at https://www.vaticannews.va/en/church/news/2024-01/rome-100-years-of-the-studium-biblicum-franciscanum-in-jerusalem.html.

164 Peter Steinfels, "Proposed Catholic Catechism Stirs Dispute Among Scholars," *The New York Times* (March 8, 1990). Available online at https://www.nytimes.com/1990/03/08/us/proposed-catholic-catechism-stirs-dispute-among-scholars.html.

165 Thomas Reese, "Greta Thunberg, a prophet for Advent," *National Catholic Reporter* (December 17, 2019). Available online at https://www.ncronline.org/news/opinion/signs-times/greta-thunberg-prophet-advent. Thomas Reese, "Pope Francis' new papal encyclical could be derailed by its seemingly sexist title," *National Catholic Reporter* (September 9, 2020). Available online at https://www.ncronline.org/vatican/signs-times/pope-

francis-new-papal-encyclical-could-be-derailed-its-seemingly-sexist-title. Thomas Reese, "It's time for a grand compromise on religious freedom and contraceptives," *National Catholic Reporter* (December 5, 2018). Available online at https://www.ncronline.org/opinion/signs-times/its-time-grand-compromise-religious-freedom-and-contraceptives.

166 Thomas Reese, "The Eucharist is about more than Christ becoming present," *National Catholic Reporter* (August 19, 2019). Available online at https://www.ncronline.org/opinion/guest-voices/signs-times/eucharist-about-more-christ-becoming-present.

167 Richard McBrien, "Perpetual Eucharistic Adoration," *National Catholic Reporter* (September 8, 2009). Available online at https://www.ncronline.org/blogs/essays-theology/perpetual-eucharistic-adoration.

168 National Council of Catholic Bishops' Committee, "Review of Fr. McBrien's *Catholicism*" (April 9, 1996). Available online at https://www.catholicculture.org/culture/library/view.cfm?id=541&CFID=121743&CFTOKEN=22026492.

169 Thomas Reese, "The Eucharist is about more than the real presence" *National Catholic Reporter* (January 31, 2023). Available online at https://www.ncronline.org/opinion/guest-voices/eucharist-about-more-real-presence.

170 Thomas Reese, "Pope Francis says no to boring homilies," *National Catholic Reporter* (April 30, 2015). Available online at https://www.ncronline.org/blogs/ncr-today/pope-francis-says-no-boring-homilies.

171 Richard McBrien, "Perpetual Eucharistic Adoration."

172 Decree on the Sacrament of the Eucharist, can. 2.

173 Jimmy Akin, "Can a Catholic Reject Transubstantiation?", Catholic Answers (February 16, 2023). Available online at https://www.catholic.com/magazine/online-edition/can-a-catholic-reject-transubstantiation.

174 Michael Sean Winters, "Weaponizing the Eucharist: The bishops, not Biden, cause scandal," *National Catholic Reporter* (May 3, 2021). Available online at https://www.ncronline.org/opinion/distinctly-catholic/weaponizing-eucharist-bishops-not-biden-cause-scandal.

175 *The Participation of Catholics in Political Life*, 4.

176 Luke Coppen, "Archbishop Cordileone bars Nancy Pelosi from Communion until she ends abortion support," *Catholic News Agency* (May 20, 2022). Available online at https://www.catholicnewsagency.com/news/251305/archbishop-cordileone-nancy-pelosi-communion-abortion.

177 Michael Sean Winters, "Weaponizing the Eucharist."

178 https://twitter.com/stevenpmillies/status/1528029549375758338.

179 "NEWS FEATURE: Abortion, Segregation Different Issues for Catholic
     Bishops," *Religion News Service* (July 27, 2004). Available online at https://
     religionnews.com/2004/07/27/news-feature-abortion-segregation-
     different-issues-for-catholic-bishops.

180 Cited in Marcellino D'Ambrosio, *When the Church Was Young: Voices of the
     Early Fathers* (Cincinnati, OH: Servant Books, 2014), 220.

181 Michael Sean Winters, "Pope Francis evangelizes very differently than US
     conservatives," *National Catholic Reporter* (December 8, 2021). Available
     online at https://www.ncronline.org/news/opinion/pope-francis-
     evangelizes-very-differently-us-conservatives.

182 John M. Vitek, "Better understanding, not apologetics, will best serve
     'nones,'" *National Catholic Reporter* (August 7, 2018). Available online at
     https://www.ncronline.org/news/people/better-understanding-not-
     apologetics-will-best-serve-nones.

183 Michael Sean Winters, "Pope Francis evangelizes very differently."

184 "Among the reasons Americans identified as important motivations in
     leaving their childhood religion are: they stopped believing in the religion's
     teachings (60 percent), their family was never that religious when they
     were growing up (32 percent), and their experience of negative religious
     teachings about or treatment of gay and lesbian people (29 percent)." Betsy
     Cooper et al., "Exodus: Why Americans are Leaving Religion—and Why
     They're Unlikely to Come Back," Public Religion Research Institute
     (September 22, 2016). Available online at https://www.prri.org/research/
     prri-rns-poll-nones-atheist-leaving-religion.

185 Chrissy Stroop, "A Note to Churches During Pride: If You're Not Lgbtq-
     Affirming, Keep Your Water," *Religion Dispatches* (June 4, 2021). Available
     online at https://religiondispatches.org/a-note-to-churches-during-pride-
     if-youre-not-lgbtq-affirming-keep-your-water.

186 Sean Swain Martin, *American Pope: Scott Hahn and the Rise of Catholic
     Fundamentalism* (Eugene, OR: Pickwick Publications, 2021), 22.

187 *Apologia Pro Vita Sua*, 4.2.

188 Matt Kappadakunnel, "We must reform and renew Catholic apologetics,"
     Where Peter Is (April 21, 2021). Available online at https://wherepeteris.
     com/we-must-reform-and-renew-catholic-apologetics.

189 "Message to Staff & Clients from Catholic Charities President & CEO Rob McCann" (June 19, 2020). Available online at https://www.youtube.com/watch?v=lKRalTfFNDo&t. The video was also covered in Daisy Zavala, "Catholic Charities video sparks controversy, highlights failures to address systemic racism," *The Spokesmen-Review* (July 7, 2020). Available online at https://www.spokesman.com/stories/2020/jul/07/catholic-charities-video-sparks-controversy-highli.

190 Patrick Reilly, "Michigan school board member facing calls to resign after tweeting 'whiteness is evil,'" *New York Post* (January 20, 2023). Available online at https://nypost.com/2023/01/20/michigan-school-board-member-slammed-for-tweeting-whiteness-is-evil.

191 Lia Eustachewich, "Coca-Cola slammed for diversity training that urged workers to be 'less white,'" *New York Post* (February 23, 2021). Available online at https://nypost.com/2021/02/23/coca-cola-diversity-training-urged-workers-to-be-less-white.

192 Charlie Brinkhurst-Cuff, "Why there's nothing racist about black-only spaces," *The Guardian* (May 30, 2017). Available online at https://www.theguardian.com/commentisfree/2017/may/30/white-people-black-women-feminist-festival.

193 Ibram X. Kendi, *How to Be an Antiracist* (New York: One World, 2019), 20.

194 Daniel P. Horan, *A White Catholic's Guide to Racism and Privilege* (Notre Dame, IN: Ave Maria Press, 2021), 10.

195 Regina Munch, "'Worship of a False God:' An Interview with Bryan Massingale," *Commonweal* (December 27, 2020). Available online at https://www.commonwealmagazine.org/worship-false-god.

196 Frank Dobbin and Alexandra Kalev, "Why Diversity Programs Fail," *Harvard Business Review* (July-August 2016). Available online at https://hbr.org/2016/07/why-diversity-programs-fail.

197 Ibram X. Kendi, *How to Be an Antiracist*, 19.

198 Renée Darline Roden, "Review: Black Lives Matter and the call to conversion," *America* (July 30, 2021). Available online at https://www.americamagazine.org/arts-culture/2021/07/30/review-birth-movement-olga-segura-241129.

199 William McGurn, "Is the Pope Capitalist?", *Wall Street Journal* (March 6, 2023). Available online at https://www.wsj.com/articles/is-the-pope-capitalist-el-pastor-francis-argentina-capitalism-free-markets-welfare-

global-south-poverty-rome-lyndon-b-johnson-social-justice-bd3de123.

200 Ibram X. Kendi, *Antiracist Baby* (New York: Kokila, 2020).

201 "The Church and Racism: Towards a More Fraternal Society." Available online at https://www.ewtn.com/catholicism/library/church-and-racism-towards-a-more-fraternal-society-2426.

202 Anna J. Marchese, "Why Bishop Barron's take on Jordan Peterson blew up on Catholic social media," *America* (June 21, 2019). Available online at https://www.americamagazine.org/faith/2019/06/21/why-bishop-barrons-take-jordan-peterson-blew-catholic-social-media.

203 Erika Rasmussen, "Amanda Gorman's Inauguration Poem Revealed God—Through Its Beauty," *America* (January 22, 2021). Available online at https://www.americamagazine.org/arts-culture/2021/01/22/amanda-gorman-biden-inauguration-poem-beauty-god-239810.

204 https://twitter.com/rightscholar/status/1355004432031895556.

205 Matt Kappadakunnel, "Birth of a Movement: The Art of Accompanying the BLM Movement," *Where Peter Is* (February 24, 2021). Available online at https://wherepeteris.com/birth-of-a-movement-the-art-of-accompanying-the-blm-movement.

206 Olga Segura, *Birth of a Movement: Black Lives Matter and the Catholic Church* (Maryknoll, NY: Orbis Books, 2021), 17. See also Kenrya Rankin, "Black Lives Matter Partners with Reproductive Justice Groups to Fight for Black Women," *Colorlines* (February 9, 2016). Available online at https://colorlines.com/article/black-lives-matter-partners-reproductive-justice-groups-fight-black-women. A now defunct campaign on the Black Lives Matter website said, "Reproductive Justice for Black Folks Starts with Expanding the Supreme Court." See https://blacklivesmatter.com/reproductive-justice-for-black-folks-starts-with-expanding-the-supreme-court/#newmode-embed-29918-40582.

207 Robert Shine, "Worcester Bishop Pens Second Letter Criticizing Pride, Black Lives Matter Flags at School," New Ways Ministry (May 7, 2022). Available online at https://www.newwaysministry.org/2022/05/07/worcester-bishop-pens-second-letter-criticizing-pride-black-lives-matter-flags-at-school.

208 Olga Segura, "This week #BlackLivesMatter turned 5. Catholics must continue to embrace its mission," *America* (July 17, 2018). Available online at https://www.americamagazine.org/politics-society/2018/07/17/week-blacklivesmatter-turned-5-catholics-must-continue-embrace-its.

209 Jamie Manson, "We all must say 'Black Lives Matter,'" *National Catholic Reporter* (June 2, 2020). Available online at https://www.ncronline.org/opinion/grace-margins/we-all-must-say-black-lives-matter.

210 Glenn Kessler, "Harris, Warren Ignore DOJ Report to claim Michael Brown was 'murdered,'" *The Washington Post* (August 13, 2019). Available online at https://www.washingtonpost.com/politics/2019/08/13/harris-warren-ignore-doj-report-claim-that-michael-brown-was-murdered.

211 Mychael Schnell, "Minnesota AG explains why Floyd's death not charged as hate crime," *The Hill* (April 25, 2021). Available online at https://thehill.com/homenews/state-watch/550211-minnesota-ag-explains-why-floyd-death-not-charged-as-hate-crime.

212 Alessandra Harris, "Are racial justice movements straying from Catholic tradition—or are Catholic leaders out of touch?", *America* (November 11, 2021). Available online at https://www.americamagazine.org/politics-society/2021/11/11/racial-justice-jose-gomez-black-catholic-241796.

213 Jennifer A Kingson, "Exclusive: $1 billion-plus riot damage is most expensive in insurance history," *Axios* (September 16, 2020). Available online at https://www.axios.com/2020/09/16/riots-cost-property-damage. This article notes the difficulty of assigning whether a death was due to the riots, but it appears that at least a dozen can be plausibly attributed to that context. Adrienne Dunne, "Fact check: More Black people died in 2019 police shootings than in George Floyd protests," *USA Today* (June 18, 2020). Available online at https://www.usatoday.com/story/news/factcheck/2020/06/18/fact-check-more-black-people-killed-police-than-floyd-protests/5323116002.

214 Aaron Morrison, "At Black Lives Matter house, families are welcomed into space of freedom and healing," AP News (November 22, 2023). Available online at https://apnews.com/article/black-lives-matter-finances-mansion-dc28cf47e3724c31d5791c90555b5b75. See also Aaron Morrison, "AP Exclusive: Black Lives Matter has $42 million in assets" AP News (May 17, 2022). Available online at https://apnews.com/article/government-and-politics-race-ethnicity-philanthropy-black-lives-matter-5bc4772e029da5220 36f8ad2a02990aa.

215 Eduardo Campos Lima, "Leonardo Boff in twitter war on liberation theology with Brazilian foreign minister," *Crux* (January 14, 2020). Available online at https://cruxnow.com/church-in-the-americas/2020/01/leonardo-boff-in-twitter-war-on-liberation-theology-

with-brazilian-foreign-minister.

216 Michael E. Lee, "After 50 years, Gutierrez's 'A Theology of Liberation' still 'What's Going On,'" *National Catholic Reporter* (December 20, 2021). Available online at https://www.ncronline.org/news/opinion/after-50-years-guti-rrezs-theology-liberation-still-whats-going.

217 David Inczauskis, "Once I discovered liberation theology, I couldn't be Catholic without it," *America* (June 4, 2021). Available online at https://www.americamagazine.org/faith/2021/06/04/liberation-theology-catholic-faith-240599.

218 *Ibid.*

219 Gustavo Gutierrez, *A Theology of Liberation: History, Politics, and Salvation* (Maryknoll, NY: Orbis Books, 1988), 17.

220 *Id.*, 60.

221 Karl Marx and Friedrich Engels, *Manifesto of the Communist Party* (1848), Chapter II. Available online at https://www.marxists.org/archive/marx/works/1848/communist-manifesto/ch02.htm.

222 Jose P. Miranda, *Communism in the Bible*, trans. Robert Barr (Eugene, OR: Wipf and Stock, 2004), 1.

223 Sobrino et al., "Rethinking Martyrdom," *Concilium* 2003/1 (London: SCM Press, 2003), 17.

224 Samuel Gregg, "Liberation Theology's Civil War," Acton Institute (July 30, 2008). Available online at https://www.acton.org/pub/commentary/2008/07/30/liberation-theologys-civil-war.

225 Gustavo Gutierrez, *A Theology of Liberation*, 110.

226 Jon Sobrino, *The True Church and the Poor* (Eugene, OR: Wipf and Stock, 2004), 95. Sobrino claims he is not "sacralizing" the poor, but in the same paragraph, he compares the poor to the sacraments as being "structural channels" for the true Church to "come into being."

227 "Notification on the Works of Father Jon Sobrino, S.J.," Congregation for the Doctrine of the Faith (November 26, 2006). Available online at https://www.vatican.va/roman_curia/congregations/cfaith/documents/rc_con_cfaith_doc_20061126_notification-sobrino_en.html.

228 "Notification on the book 'Church: Charism and Power' by Father Leonardo Boff, O.F.M.*," Congregation for the Doctrine of the Faith (March 11, 1985). Available online at https://www.vatican.va/roman_curia/congregations/cfaith/documents/rc_con_cfaith_doc_19850311_

notif-boff_en.html.

229 Francis X. Rocca, Luciana Magalhaes, and Samantha Pearson, "The Catholic Church Is Losing Latin America," *The Wall Street Journal* (January 11, 2022). Available online at https://www.wsj.com/articles/why-the-catholic-church-is-losing-latin-america-11641914388.

230 Daniel H. Levine, "Protestants and Catholics in Latin America: A Family Portrait," *Fundamentalisms Comprehended*, eds. Martin E. Marty and R. Scott Appleby (Chicago: University of Chicago Press, 2004), 160.

231 "Instruction on Christian Freedom and Liberation," Congregation for the Doctrine of the Faith (March 22, 1986), 22, 98. Available online at https://www.vatican.va/roman_curia/congregations/cfaith/documents/rc_con_cfaith_doc_19860322_freedom-liberation_en.html.

232 Leonardo Boff, *Francis of Rome and Francis of Assisi: A New Springtime for the Church* (Maryknoll, NY: Orbis Books, 2014), 76.

233 Dean Dettloff, "Is Pope Francis a Liberation Theologian?", *Sojourners* (October 26, 2021). Available online at https://sojo.net/articles/pope-francis-liberation-theologian.

234 "Only in Christ Will Man Find Total Salvation." Available online at https://www.vatican.va/jubilee_2000/magazine/documents/ju_mag_01041998_p-26_en.html#:~:text=Jesus%20comes%20to%20offer%20us,complete%20fulfilment%20of%20our%20destiny.

235 "Voyage of the St. Louis." Available online at https://encyclopedia.ushmm.org/content/en/article/voyage-of-the-st-louis.

236 Rachel Amiri, "Deportation is evil," *Where Peter Is* (September 24, 2021). Available online at https://wherepeteris.com/deportation-is-evil.

237 Darren M. Henson, "Deportation: A Moral Morass," *Health Progress* (July-August 2017). Available online at https://www.chausa.org/publications/health-progress/article/july-august-2017/deportation-a-moral-morass.

238 Chelsey Cox, "Are Haitian migrants being deported, repatriated or expelled? And what's the difference?", *USA Today* (September 23, 2021). Available online at https://www.usatoday.com/story/news/politics/2021/09/23/deportation-expulsion-repatriation-whats-difference/5830081001.

239 Jimmy Akin, "Is Deportation Intrinsically Evil?", Catholic Answers (July 18, 2018). Available online at https://www.catholic.com/magazine/online-edition/is-deportation-intrinsically-evil.

240 "Address of His Holiness Pius XII to the Members of the United States Senate of the Committee on Immigration" (October 31, 1947). Available online at https://www.vatican.va/content/pius-xii/en/speeches/1947/documents/hf_p-xii_spe_19471031_senatori-usa.html.

241 John Paul II, General Audience (November 15, 1978). Available online at https://www.vatican.va/content/john-paul-ii/en/audiences/1978/documents/hf_jp-ii_aud_19781115.html.

242 John Paul II, Address of the Holy Father (June 23, 2001). Available online at https://www.vatican.va/content/john-paul-ii/en/speeches/2001/june/documents/hf_jp-ii_spe_20010623_ucraina-meeting.html.

243 Pope Francis, "Press Conference on the Return Flight from Tallin (Estonia) to Rome" (September 25, 2018). Available online at https://www.vatican.va/content/francesco/en/speeches/2018/september/documents/papa-francesco_20180925_voloritorno-estonia.html.

244 Darren M. Henson, "Deportation: A Moral Morass."

245 "In-Flight Press Conference of His Holiness Pope Francis from Mexico To Rome" (February 17, 2016). Available online at https://www.vatican.va/content/francesco/en/speeches/2016/february/documents/papa-francesco_20160217_messico-conferenza-stampa.html.

246 "Press Conference of His Holiness Pope Francis on the Return Flight from Colombia To Rome" (September 10, 2017). Available online at https://www.vatican.va/content/francesco/en/speeches/2017/september/documents/papa-francesco_20170910_viaggioapostolico-colombia-voloritorno.html.

247 "Editorial: The new gun control law is good. Now, let's do an assault weapons ban," *National Catholic Reporter* (July 14, 2022). Available online at https://www.ncronline.org/news/opinion/editorial-new-gun-control-law-good-now-lets-do-assault-weapons-ban.

248 Jimmy Akin, "What Does the Church Say About Gun Control?", Catholic Answers (February 25, 2016). Available online at https://www.catholic.com/magazine/online-edition/what-does-the-church-say-about-gun-control.

249 Lydia O'Kane, "Texas shootings: Pope condemns indiscriminate trafficking of arms," *Vatican News* (May 2022). Available online at https://www.vaticannews.va/en/pope/news/2022-05/pope-francis-heartbroken-at-latest-us-shooting.html.

250 "Vatican council issues report favoring handgun controls," *Tampa Bay*

Times (June 24, 1994). Jimmy Akin notes that this passage is found in "The International Arms Trade: An Ethical Reflection," a 1994 document by the Pontifical Commission for Justice and Peace (PCJP), under the heading "Furnishing Arms to Groups That Are Not States." See Akin, "What Does the Church Say About Gun Control?"

251 Carol Glatz, "Gun control: Church firmly, quietly opposes firearms for civilians," *National Catholic Reporter* (January 14, 2011). Available online at https://www.ncronline.org/gun-control-church-firmly-quietly-opposes-firearms-civilians.

252 Thomas A. Shannon, "The Idolatry of Weapons," *America* (July 24, 2012). Available online at https://www.americamagazine.org/content/all-things/idolatry-weapons. Concerning abortion, Shannon and his co-author Allan Wolter say human embryos are not fully human because of their high mortality rate. They say it is almost "sacrilegious" to claim this due to the "bungling" it implies on the part of an all-wise Creator. Thomas A. Shannon and Allan B. Wolter, "Reflections on the Moral Status of the Pre-Embryo," *Theological Studies* (December 1990), 619.

253 Thomas Reese, "America sacramentalizes guns as God's gift to the good. This is heresy," *National Catholic Reporter* (December 1, 2021). Available online at https://www.ncronline.org/news/justice/america-sacramentalizes-guns-gods-gift-good-heresy.

254 Michael Sean Winters, "Bring back the assault weapons ban," *National Catholic Reporter* (March 29, 2021). Available online at https://www.ncronline.org/news/distinctly-catholic/bring-back-assault-weapons-ban.

255 "Do they fire particularly powerful rifle ammunition? No. In fact the AR-15 is illegal for deer hunting in many places because it tends to use very low-powered ammunition." James Fallows, "Why Stop With the AR-15?", *The Atlantic* (March 5, 2018). Available online at https://www.theatlantic.com/politics/archive/2018/03/the-case-against-gun-control-cont/622285.

256 "Weapon types used in mass shootings in the United States between 1982 and April 2023, by number of weapons and incidents." Available online at https://www.statista.com/statistics/476409/mass-shootings-in-the-us-by-weapon-types-used.

257 This figure is based on the The Associated Press's reporting of 175 deaths since the Columbine shooting twenty-three years ago. "Mass school shootings kill 175 from Columbine to Nashville," The Associated Press (March 27,

2023). Available online at https://apnews.com/article/nashville-mass-school-shooting-database-columbine-uvalde-1c82749f7236752a2e621f402489b357.

258 Max Kapustin et al., "Gun Violence in Chicago, 2016," University of Chicago Crime Lab (January 2017). Available online at https://urbanlabs.uchicago.edu/attachments/c5b0b0b86b6b6a9309ed88a9f5bbe5bd892d4077/store/82f93d3e7c7cc4c5a29abca0d8bf5892b3a35c0c3253d1d24b3b9d1fa7b8/UChicagoCrimeLab+Gun+Violence+in+Chicago+2016.pdf.

259 "TIME's examination of the deadliest recent mass shootings showed it was difficult to point to cases where more expansive background checks would have saved lives. Many of the people who perpetrated these mass shootings passed background checks." Tara Law, "Background Checks Won't Stop Many Mass Shootings. We Need Them Anyway, Experts Say," *Time Magazine* (August 10, 2019). Available online at https://time.com/5648987/mass-shootings-background-checks.

260 Rhitu Chatterjee, "Mass shootings can be contagious, research shows," National Public Radio (January 24, 2023). Available online at https://www.npr.org/sections/health-shots/2019/08/06/748767807/mass-shootings-can-be-contagious-research-shows.

261 Jeff Jacoby, "The Very Racist History of Gun Control," *Boston Globe* (July 31, 2021). Available online at https://www.bostonglobe.com/2021/07/31/opinion/very-racist-history-gun-control.

262 Robert David Sullivan, "Voting Catholic: Is there a Catholic approach to gun policy?", *America* (October 31, 2022). Available online at https://www.americamagazine.org/politics-society/2022/10/31/voting-catholic-2022-guns-244037.

263 "A CDC-sponsored study from 2013 found that 'guns are used in self-defense anywhere from 500,000 to 3 million times a year,' Pratt said. 'That means that compared to the CDC figures for "firearm homicides" in 2016, guns are being used 35 to 208 times more often to save [lives].'" Susan Scutti, "Gun homicides on the rise, CDC says," CNN.com (July 26, 2018). Available online at https://www.cnn.com/2018/07/26/health/common-methods-of-homicide-cdc/index.html. It appears that in 2022, the CDC removed links to this study after complaints from gun control advocates but never officially retracted the study. Anders Hagstrom, "CDC removed stats on defensive gun use over pressure from gun control activists: report,"

Fox News (December 15, 2022). Available online at https://www.foxnews.com/politics/cdc-removed-stats-defensive-gun-use-pressure-gun-control-activists-report.

264 William English, "2021 National Firearms Survey," Georgetown McDonough School of Business Research Paper no. 3887145 (July 16, 2021). Available online at https://papers.ssrn.com/sol3/papers.cfm?abstract_id=3887145.

265 Joe Dantona, "Cardinal Müller is Disturbingly Wrong on Climate Change," *Where Peter Is* (November 18, 2019). Available online at https://wherepeteris.com/cardinal-muller-is-disturbingly-wrong-on-climate-change.

266 Doug Demeo, "Getting Out of Oil: Catholic universities can make a difference through divestment," *America* (April 9, 2014). Available online at https://www.americamagazine.org/issue/getting-out-oil.

267 Brian Roewe, "Vatican official: Church divestment from fossil fuels is 'moral imperative,'" *National Catholic Reporter* (May 20, 2021). Available online at https://www.ncronline.org/earthbeat/vatican-official-church-divestment-fossil-fuels-moral-imperative.

268 "Editorial: Why have no US Catholic dioceses divested from fossil fuels?", *National Catholic Reporter* (May 2, 2023). Available online at https://www.ncronline.org/opinion/editorial/editorial-why-have-no-us-catholic-dioceses-divested-fossil-fuels. In 2024, San Diego became the first American diocese to divest from fossil fuels. Brian Roewe, "In first for US church, San Diego Diocese divests from fossil fuels," *National Catholic Reporter* (January 12, 2024). Available online at https://www.ncronline.org/earthbeat/faith/first-us-church-san-diego-diocese-divests-fossil-fuels.

269 Thomas Reese, "COVID-19, global warming and diminishing Catholic guilt," *National Catholic Reporter* (May 20, 2021). Available online at https://www.ncronline.org/earthbeat/justice/covid-19-global-warming-and-diminishing-catholic-guilt.

270 Daniel R. Dileo, "Study: Most US Catholic bishops kept silent on Francis' climate change push," *National Catholic Reporter* (October 19, 2021). Available online at https://www.ncronline.org/earthbeat/politics/study-most-us-catholic-bishops-kept-silent-francis-climate-change-push.

271 Jimmy Akin, *Teaching with Authority: How to Cut Through Doctrinal Confusion and Understand What the Church Really Says* (El Cajon, CA: Catholic Answers Press, 2018), 123.

272 Matthew Sitman, "Preeminent?"

273 Malcolm Schluenderfritz, "Sacrificing to Protect our Common Home," *Where Peter Is* (April 22, 2022). Available online at https://wherepeteris. com/sacrificing-to-protect-our-common-home.

274 Matthew E. Kahn et al., "Long-Term Macroeconomic Effects of Climate Change: A Cross-Country Analysis," International Monetary Fund (October 2019). Available online at https://www.imf.org/-/media/Files/ Publications/WP/2019/wpiea2019215-print-pdf.ashx. Swiss Re gives a higher prediction of 18 percent GDP loss by 2100. See https://www. swissre.com/media/press-release/nr-20210422-economics-of-climate-change-risks.html.

275 Thomas Reese, "Commentary: Abortion preeminent issue, global warming not urgent, say bishops," *Salt Lake Tribune* (November 14, 2019). Available online at https://www.sltrib.com/religion/2019/11/14/commentary-abortion.

276 "Climate Change and Health," World Health Organization (October 30, 2021). Available online at https://www.who.int/news-room/fact-sheets/ detail/climate-change-and-health. R. Daniel Bressler, "The mortality cost of carbon," *Nature Communications*, vol. 12, no. 4467 (July 29, 2021). Available online at https://www.nature.com/articles/s41467-021-24487-w.

277 Harry Stevens, "Will global warming make temperature less deadly?", *The Washington Post* (February 16, 2023). Available online at https://www. washingtonpost.com/climate-environment/interactive/2023/hot-cold-extreme-temperature-deaths.

278 See https://ourworldindata.org/co2/country/united-states vs. https:// ourworldindata.org/co2/country/china.

279 Shaner et al., "Geophysical constraints on the reliability of solar and wind power in the United States," *Energy Environmental Science*, vol. 11, no. 4 (2018), 914–925.

280 This is assuming that $175 billion is spent annually for twenty years. See Jeffrey Sachs, *The End of Poverty: Economic Possibilities for Our Time* (New York: Penguin Books, 2015), 299.

281 Malcolm Schluenderfritz, "Opposing Culture, or Opposing an Anti-Culture?", *Where Peter Is* (July 2, 2021). Available online at https:// wherepeteris.com/opposing-culture-or-opposing-an-anti-culture.

282 Kevin Mortimer et al. "A cleaner burning biomass-fueled cookstove intervention to prevent pneumonia in children under five years old in

rural Malawi (the Cooking and Pneumonia Study): a cluster randomised controlled trial," *Lancet* 14;389 (2017). Available online at https://pubmed.ncbi.nlm.nih.gov/27939058.

283 Todd Moss et al. "The Modern Energy Minimum: The case for a new global electricity consumption threshold," *Energy for Growth Hub* (September 30, 2020). Available online at https://www.rockefellerfoundation.org/wp-content/uploads/2020/12/Modern-Energy-Minimum-Sept30.pdf.

284 "Japan confirms first Fukushima worker death from radiation," BBC News (September 5, 2018). Available online at https://www.bbc.com/news/world-asia-45423575.

285 Christopher Wells, "Pope Francis: A world free of nuclear weapons is necessary and possible," *Vatican News* (June 21, 2022). Available online at https://www.vaticannews.va/en/pope/news/2022-06/pope-francis-a-world-free-of-nuclear-weapons-is-necessary.html.

286 Nick Touran, "Nuclear fuel will last us for 4 billion years," *What is nuclear energy?* (October 28, 2020). Available online at https://whatisnuclear.com/nuclear-sustainability.html.

287 Chris Baraniuk, "Weird 'wind drought' means Britain's turbines are at a standstill," *New Scientist* (July 17, 2018). Available online at https://www.newscientist.com/article/2174262-weird-wind-drought-means-britains-turbines-are-at-a-standstill.

288 Kristin Shrader-Frechette, "Five Myths About Nuclear Energy," *America* (June 23, 2008). Available online at https://www.americamagazine.org/issue/660/article/five-myths-about-nuclear-energy.

289 Thomas Bruckner et al. "Annex III: Technology-specific cost and performance parameters," in "Climate Change 2014: Mitigation of Climate Change. Contribution of Working Group III to the Fifth Assessment Report of the Intergovernmental Panel on Climate Change" (2014). Available online at https://www.ipcc.ch/site/assets/uploads/2018/02/ipcc_wg3_ar5_annex-iii.pdf#page=7.

290 "Electricity explained: Electricity generation, capacity, and sales in the United States," U.S. Energy Information Administration (July 15, 2022). Available online at https://www.eia.gov/energyexplained/electricity/electricity-in-the-us-generation-capacity-and-sales.php.

291 "Nuclear power plants generated 68 percent of France's electricity in 2021," U.S. Energy Information Administration (January 23,

2023). Available online at https://www.eia.gov/todayinenergy/detail.
php?id=55259#.

292 Peter Steinfels, "Reinventing Liberal Catholicism," *Commonweal Magazine*
(June 17, 2004). Available online at https://www.commonwealmagazine.
org/reinventing-liberal-catholicism.

293 See for example John Finnis, Robert P. George, and Peter Ryan, "More
Confusion About Same-sex Blessings," *First Things* (January 15, 2024).
Available online at https://www.firstthings.com/web-exclusives/2024/01/
more-confusion-about-same-sex-blessings.

294 Courtney Mares, "Vatican responds to widespread backlash on same-sex
blessing directive" *Catholic News Agency* (January 4, 2024). Available online
at https://www.catholicnewsagency.com/news/256439/vatican-responds-
to-widespread-backlash-on-same-sex-blessing-directive.

295 Philip Pullella, "Pope says LGBT blessings are for individuals, not approval
of unions," *Reuters* (January 26, 2024). Available online at https://www.
reuters.com/world/europe/pope-says-lgbt-blessings-are-individuals-not-
approval-unions-2024-01-26.

296 Amy Harmon, Ruth Graham, and Sarah Maslan Nir, "Making History
on a Tuesday Morning, with the Church's Blessing," *The New York
Times* (December 21, 2023). Available online at https://www.nytimes.
com/2023/12/19/us/catholic-gay-blessing-pope-francis.html.

297 Michael F. Pettinger, "Why LGBTQ Catholics Are Ambivalent About
the 'Gift' of Same-Sex Blessings," *The Nation* (January 3, 2024). Available
online at: https://www.thenation.com/article/archive/same-sex-blessing-
catholic-francis.

298 Robert Shine, "Top Cardinal Retracts Previous Call for Revision of
Church Teaching on Homosexuality," New Ways Ministry (September 2,
2022). Available online at https://www.newwaysministry.org/2022/09/02/
top-cardinal-retracts-previous-call-for-revision-of-church-teaching-on-
homosexuality.

299 *Building a Bridge* (2021). The relevant clip can be seen in my review of the
film at "My review of Fr. James Martin's new documentary." Available
online at https://www.youtube.com/watch?v=n9TrCqiyi_Q.

300 Francis George, "How Liberalism Fails the Church," *Commonweal Magazine*
(June 17, 2004). Available online at https://www.commonwealmagazine.
org/how-liberalism-fails-church.